JAPAN
in Pictures

VGS

Alison Behnke

Lerner Publications Company

Contents

INTRODUCTION   4

THE LAND   8

▶ Rivers and Lakes. Climate. Flora and Fauna. Cities.

HISTORY AND GOVERNMENT   20

▶ Prehistory. Chinese Influence. Fujiwara Leadership. Kamakura Period. The Ashikaga Shogunate. The 1600s to 1867. The Meiji Restoration. Japanese Imperialism. World War I and World War II. Military Occupation. Postwar Boom. Troubled Economy. Government.

THE PEOPLE   38

▶ Ethnic Background. Language. Social Structure. Marriage and Family. Education. Health.

Website address: www.lernerbooks.com

Lerner Publications Company
A division of Lerner Publishing Group
241 First Avenue North
Minneapolis, MN 55401 U.S.A.

web enhanced @ www.vgsbooks.com

CULTURAL LIFE 48

► Religion. Holidays and Festivals. Literature.
Drama and Music. Visual Arts and Multimedia.
Sports. Food and Dress.

THE ECONOMY 58

► Manufacturing. Foreign Trade. Agriculture.
Fishing. Transportation. The Future.

FOR MORE INFORMATION

► Timeline 66
► Fast Facts 68
► Currency 68
► Flag 69
► National Anthem 69
► Famous People 70
► Sights to See 72
► Glossary 73
► Selected Bibliography 74
► Further Reading and Websites 76
► Index 78

Library of Congress Cataloging-in-Publication Data

Behnke, Alison.
    Japan in pictures / by Alison Behnke.—Rev. and expanded.
        p.   cm. — (Visual geography series)
    ISBN: 0-8225-1956-9 (lib. bdg. : alk. paper)
    1. Japan—Pictorial works—Juvenile literature. 2. Japan—Juvenile literature. I. Title. II. Series.
    DS806.B425 2003
    952—dc21   2001002955

Manufactured in the United States of America
1 2 3 4 5 6 - JR - 08 07 06 05 04 03

INTRODUCTION

Rising from the waters of the Pacific Ocean east of the Asian mainland, the island nation of Japan holds more than ten thousand years of history within its small territory. Japan is a land of many facets and contrasts, from prehistoric pottery to towering modern skyscrapers, and from fertile coastal plains to steep and snowy mountains. Yet the inhabitants of this diverse country also have a strong sense of national identity, pride, and tradition. The Japanese know their country as Nihon or Nippon (Land of the Rising Sun).

Japan has operated as an isolated realm throughout much of its history, keeping its contact with other nations to a minimum. But the Japanese people have demonstrated a unique ability to adopt and reshape outside influences to fit their own needs and values. For example, when Chinese culture entered Japan around the A.D. 400s, the Japanese borrowed Chinese patterns of government, education, art, and religion. As they adopted these cultural elements, the Japanese also gradually molded them into distinct Japanese forms.

Although external contact continued to be limited, frequent— and often fierce—internal struggles raged in Japan beginning around the early A.D. 800s. Emperors, aristocratic families, and powerful warlords vied for control of the country during this tumultuous period. Amidst the upheaval, Japanese authors, artists, and scholars continued to produce novels, poetry, paintings, and other works. Agriculture and commerce also advanced, and external trade began to establish ties between Japan and other nations between the fourteenth and sixteenth centuries.

Despite the growing export of Japanese goods, Japan's leaders remained wary of interaction with other countries in the 1600s and 1700s, and the nation's isolation became more pronounced. After a new, more outward looking government came to power in the nineteenth century, Japan officially reopened to international contact in 1868. This shift marked the beginning of the Meiji Restoration, during which Japanese leaders sought to modernize their country.

As in the past, the Japanese people quickly adopted new ideas from the outside world, including principles of modern technology, and the country set out to become a major global power. After the destruction of almost every Japanese industrial center during World War II (1939–1945), the nation made a rapid recovery. By the last quarter of the twentieth century, Japan had become an international economic leader. However, Japan's powerful economy began to falter in the 1990s due to rising interest rates and falling prices for Japanese goods. In the early 2000s, the nation is still struggling to recover from a serious economic recession as its leaders look for answers to banking problems, unemployment, and homelessness.

The Japanese live in a modern industrial society, yet they retain ancient customs. Drawing on a rich artistic heritage, many Japanese continue to practice and produce traditional art forms. At the same time, modern Japanese artists explore new styles and themes for creative expression. Long-held patterns of social behavior are still honored and have been adapted to modern business as part of highly successful management techniques. This firm grounding in both the past and the present plays a key role in Japan's strength and stability, and in its future as a nation.

CHINA RUSSIA

SAKHALIN
ISLAND
[RUSSIA]

SEA OF
OKHOTSK

Japan

⊛ Capital city
• City
— International border

0   200 Miles
0   200 KM

N

Teshio R.

Ishikari R.

Tokachi R.

• Sapporo

HOKKAIDO

NORTH
KOREA

SEA OF
JAPAN

Kitakami R.

Mogami R.

SOUTH
KOREA

Shinano River

Lake
Inawashiro

Lake Chuzenji

Abukuma R.

HONSHU

Tokyo
Kawasaki
Yokohama Chiba
Kamakura

NORTH
PACIFIC
OCEAN

Tone R.

Lake
Biwa

Kiso River

Nagoya

Korea Strait

Kyoto

Himeji

Kobe
Nara

Osaka

Tokyo Bay

Okayama

Hiroshima Kure

INLAND
SEA

Yoshino
River

Ise Bay

Shimonoseki

Fukuoka Kitakyushu

Matsuyama

Chikugo R.

Osaka Bay

SHIKOKU

Nagasaki

KYUSHU

Kagoshima

EAST
CHINA
SEA

RYUKYU ISLANDS

KURIL ISLANDS

JAPAN

NORTH
PACIFIC
OCEAN

RYUKYU ISLANDS

OKINAWA

BONIN ISLANDS

0   200 Miles
0   200 KM

THE LAND

Lying across the Sea of Japan from China, Russia, and North and South Korea, Japan consists of a roughly crescent-shaped chain of islands midway between the equator and the North Pole. From northeast to southwest, the country extends approximately 1,300 miles (2,092 kilometers), and its widest section spans about 200 miles (322 km).

From north to south, the largest of the islands are Hokkaido, Honshu, Shikoku, and Kyushu. Honshu, the biggest of the four, contains most of Japan's major cities—Tokyo, Yokohama, Osaka, Kyoto, and Kobe. Thousands of smaller islands lie off the shores of the larger land-masses. The country's territory also includes the Ryukyu and Bonin island chains to the south. Russia's Kuril Islands lie to the northeast.

Japan has a land area of about 145,000 square miles (375,550 sq. km), making it nearly the size of the state of Montana. To the north sits the Sea of Okhotsk, and to the east and south lie the North Pacific Ocean and the East China Sea, respectively. To the west, the

Korea Strait and the Sea of Japan separate the country from China, North and South Korea, and Russia.

A chain of mountains forms Japan's backbone, running lengthwise down the middle of all the islands. Created by the slow collision of two tectonic plates, or sections of the earth's crust, the mountains of Japan are still taking form. Severe earthquakes strike every few years, and minor tremors are an almost daily occurrence. Tidal waves or tsunami—unusually high sea waves—frequently accompany earthquakes along the eastern coast. Japan has about two hundred volcanoes, and more than sixty are active.

Much of Japan is naturally forested, and parts of the country have rich soil for farming. However, the land's mountainous topography makes these resources difficult to draw upon. Japan also has a wide variety of natural mineral resources, but only in small quantities. As a result, Japan imports most of its raw materials, as well as a significant amount of its food.

CHINA

RUSSIA

SAKHALIN
ISLAND
(RUSSIA)

SEA OF
OKHOTSK

Japan

Feet	Meters	
9843	3000	Mountains
6582	2000	Uplands
3281	1000	
1640	500	Lowlands

Elevation

N

——— International border
▲ Highest point

0   200 Miles
0   200 KM

NORTH
KOREA

ISHIKARI
MTNS.

Kushiro
Plain

HIDAKA
MTNS.

Teshio R.

Ishikari R.

Tokachi R.

Oshima
Peninsula

HOKKAIDO

SEA OF
JAPAN

SOUTH
KOREA

HONSHU

Kitakami R.

Sendai
Plain

Mogami R.

Niigata Plain

Shinano River

Lake
Inawashiro

Lake Chuzenji

Tone R.

Kinu R.

JAPANESE
ALPS

Fujiyama
(Mount Fuji)
▲

Kanto
Plain

Cape Inubo

NORTH
PACIFIC
OCEAN

Korea Strait

Lake Biwa

Kiso River

Osaka
Plain

Ise Bay

Tokyo Bay

INLAND SEA

Yoshino
River

Kii Peninsula

SHIKOKU
MTNS.

Osaka Bay

SHIKOKU

Chikugo R.

KYUSHU MTNS.

KYUSHU

EAST
CHINA
SEA

RYUKYU ISLANDS

KURIL ISLANDS

JAPAN

NORTH
PACIFIC
OCEAN

BONIN ISLANDS

RYUKYU ISLANDS

OKINAWA

0   200 Miles
0   200 KM

Japanese women work in a **rice paddy.** Mount Fuji looms in the background.

HONSHU Although mountains cover most of Honshu, about 80 percent of Japan's 127 million people live on this island. Most of the population at the northern end of the island live in small valleys that separate three mountain ranges. Fertile soil makes agriculture the primary occupation in this region. Along the Pacific Ocean at the southern end of these northern mountains lies the Sendai Plain. The Niigata Plain extends west of the mountains to the Sea of Japan.

The Japanese Alps, the country's tallest mountains, dominate the landscape of central Honshu. To the east, a chain of volcanoes cuts through the center of the island. Fujiyama (or Mount Fuji), an inactive volcano in this chain, is Japan's highest peak (12,388 feet or 3,776 meters). Farther east, the mountains descend into the Kanto Plain, Japan's largest lowland region. The Kanto Plain, which is the site of the nation's capital city of Tokyo, is an important agricultural and industrial center. To the south and west, the Osaka Plain produces much of the nation's food and is the location of many manufacturing plants.

Mount Fuji, Japan's national landmark, was once considered too sacred for any but priests and religious travelers, but the mountain and the five lakes at its base are now open to everyone. Thousands of people make the hike to Fuji's peak every year. Viewing the rising sun from the summit is especially popular.

Mountains make up most of southwestern Honshu, although small lowlands are scattered throughout the region. Local inhabitants fish, farm, or work in industrial cities to earn a living.

HOKKAIDO Hokkaido, Japan's second largest island, lies north of Honshu and contains less than 5 percent of the population. Forested mountains and hills cover much of Hokkaido. The central Ishikari Mountains meet a north-south chain known as the Hidaka Mountains.

A large plain drained by the Ishikari River lies northeast of the Oshima Peninsula in the southwest. Smaller lowland areas, such as the Kushiro Plain, border the eastern coast. The main occupations on Hokkaido are dairy farming, fishing, and forestry. The island's northern setting makes winter sports a popular recreation.

KYUSHU Kyushu is the southernmost of Japan's main islands, and home to about 11 percent of the population. The steep, heavily forested Kyushu Mountains run down the center of the island. The northwest contains rolling hills and wide plains that have been developed into an urban industrial area. In the west lies Kyushu's main

A farmer carries milking equipment through a barn. Hokkaido's lush lowland areas make ideal spots for dairy farms.

Bathers enjoy a nice, relaxing soak in one of **Japan's natural hot springs.** For links to more hot springs information, go to vgsbooks.com.

agricultural district and largest lowland.

Volcanoes, high lava plateaus, and large deposits of volcanic ash exist at the northeastern and southern ends of the island. Only small areas along the coasts and inland can be cultivated. To maximize the amount of land available for growing crops, farmers terrace the steep hillsides by cutting out level strips of land from the sides of plateaus.

SHIKOKU The smallest of Japan's main islands, Shikoku contains just over 3 percent of the population. Mountains cover much of the center of the landmass, and most of the island's inhabitants live in the north near the coast of the Inland Sea. Miners extract copper in northern Shikoku, and the fertile soil that borders the Inland Sea is cultivated by farmers growing rice and fruit. Farmers on the narrow plain of Shikoku's southern coast also raise rice and other crops.

NATURAL SPAS

The geothermal activity beneath Japan's surface that causes earthquakes and volcanic eruptions has also dotted the nation with hot mineral springs, or *onsen*. Many of these springs, believed to have health benefits, have been made into indoor pools, while others remain outside. People enjoy these natural spas, and, in the winter, so do some animals—Japanese snow monkeys occasionally warm up in the hot springs of the north.

Much of **Japan's coastline is scattered with tiny islands** jutting out of the ocean.

THE RYUKYU AND BONIN ISLANDS With more than one hundred islands—the most important of which is Okinawa—the Ryukyus stretch south from Kyushu to Taiwan and separate the East China Sea from the Pacific Ocean. Formed by the peaks of submerged mountains, this island chain contains active volcanoes. Although some of the islands are uninhabited, the entire chain has more than 1 million people.

The Bonin Islands lie in the Pacific Ocean, east of the Ryukyus and about 600 miles (965 km) southeast of Honshu. Covering only 41 square miles (106 sq. km), the Bonins contain fewer than 2,500 people, most of whom are farmers. These islands are rocky, and tall grass and scrub trees cover the land.

Rivers and Lakes

Japan has many short, swift rivers, most of which begin in the mountains and flow through deep valleys. The amount of water flowing in these rivers changes depending on the season and the weather. Because the riverbeds are narrow and short, water overflows their banks during long rainy periods, and droughts occur when little rain falls.

Although inland rivers are not large enough to be used for transportation, they are a primary source of water and hydroelectric energy. Some of the rivers have fertile plains, or deltas, at their mouths, where they empty into shallow, sheltered bays. These plains have been heavily farmed for centuries. Most of Japan's population live in the many cities that have been built on these fertile deltas.

Over the centuries, the Gokase River cut a deep channel through lava formations, creating the **stunning Takachiho Gorge** on the island of Kyushu.

Only two rivers in Japan exceed 200 miles (322 km) in length. They are the Shinano, whose mouth forms Honshu's Niigata Plain, and the Ishikari, which drains the Ishikari Plain on western Hokkaido. Other rivers on Honshu include the Kiso, Tone, Kinu, Mogami, and Kitakami. In addition to the Ishikari, the Teshio and Tokachi also water Hokkaido. The longest rivers on Shikoku and Kyushu are the Yoshino and Chikugo, respectively. Numerous smaller streams flow through almost every valley in the country. Japan also has many scenic lakes—such as Biwa, Chuzenji, and Inawashiro—which are located primarily in mountainous regions.

Climate

Because of the length of the Japanese island chain, Japan's climate varies considerably from place to place. In addition, monsoons (moisture-bearing seasonal winds) and ocean currents affect the weather.

In the north, on Hokkaido, summers are cool, averaging below 70°F (21°C), and winters are severe, with heavy snowfall and average temperatures below 20°F (-7°C). Honshu has warm, humid summers with temperatures in the 70s (21°C–26°C) and, along the southern coast, in the 80s (26°C–32°C). Winters on Honshu are mild in the south and cold and snowy in the north, where the climate is more like that on Hokkaido. Kyushu and Shikoku

Hokkaido's white winters make Sapporo, its biggest city, the perfect place for a snow festival (Yuki Matsuri). Each February hundreds of ice and snow sculptures appear in Sapporo's main park and streets, drawing visitors from all over the world.

Only the **foundations of houses remained** on the coast after this Japanese town was struck by a devastating tsunami.

have long, hot summers—temperatures in the 80s (26°C–32°C) are common—and mild winters with temperatures rarely dropping below the freezing point.

Two Pacific Ocean currents moderate the weather in Japan. The warm Kuroshio (Japan) Current flows northward along the southern and eastern coasts up to Tokyo, where it turns east. The Oyashio Current carries cold water southward along the eastern coasts of Hokkaido and northern Honshu.

Monsoons also influence Japan's climate and seasonal weather. In the winter, a monsoon from the northwest carries cold air and snow to northern Japan. In the summer, a monsoon blows warm, moist air from the southeast, causing hot, humid weather in southern and central Japan.

Japan's abundant annual rainfall varies from 45 to 75 inches (114 to 191 centimeters), except on eastern Hokkaido, which is drier than the rest of the country. Western Japan, facing the Sea of Japan, usually receives heavier rainfall than the Pacific side does. Two rainy seasons occur, from mid-June to early July and from September to October. In late summer and early fall, floods and typhoons (Pacific hurricanes) often lash the islands and can severely damage houses, crops, and shipping facilities.

Flora and Fauna

Thousands of species of plants thrive in the warm, humid climate of Japan. The Japanese particularly admire the blossoming of cherry and plum trees in early spring. Numerous flower festivals are held around the country, and many Japanese cultivate plants that bloom throughout the growing season.

Natural vegetation consists almost entirely of forests, which cover nearly three-quarters of the country. Temperature and altitude determine the boundaries of Japan's three forest zones. Hokkaido contains boreal (subarctic) forests, which include fir, spruce, larch, birch, alder, and aspen. On northern and central Honshu, trees such as maple, beech, willow, chestnut, poplar, oak, cypress, yew, holly, and mulberry are abundant. On Kyushu, Shikoku, and southern Honshu, subtropical camphor and wax trees thrive, as do bamboo and cultivated tea plants.

Japan's animal life is not as abundant as its vegetation is. Yet many species of mammals live on the islands, along with hundreds of different kinds of birds and a variety of reptiles, amphibians, and fish. Mammals include Japanese macaques (snow monkeys), bears, foxes, badgers, mink, otters, weasels, seals, rabbits, and various rodents. Sparrows, house swallows, and thrushes are the most common birds. Water birds—cranes, herons, ducks, cormorants, and storks, for example—and songbirds are also common.

Japanese macaque

Japan's coastal waters abound with fish. Fishing crews catch huge quantities, which are eaten fresh, canned, or used as fertilizer. The meeting point of the Kuroshio and Oyashio Currents on Honshu's eastern coast of is a particularly bountiful fishing area.

JAPAN'S CHERRY BLOSSOMS

The cherry blossom, or *sakura*, is one of Japan's most beloved national symbols. With its delicate petals and its short time in bloom—often only a week—the flower has a variety of meanings to the Japanese, including beauty, purity, and the fleeting nature of earthly existence. Each spring, as the "cherry blossom front" (*sakura zensen*) moves northward, people all over Japan gather for parties and picnics under the trees. Visit vgsbooks.com for links to additional information on the celebration of cherry blossoms.

Cities

Japan's capital and largest city is Tokyo, with approximately 8 million inhabitants in the city itself and more than 11.7 million in the Tokyo Metropolitan Prefecture (Tokyo-to). One of the largest urban areas in the world, Tokyo is the hub of Japanese culture, education, economy, and transportation. Until 1868, when Tokyo became the nation's capital, the city was known as Edo.

Because the capital is so large, the problems that face most world cities are compounded in Tokyo. Due to a severe shortage of housing, living quarters in Tokyo are expensive. Many people live in distant suburbs far from where they work. Transportation facilities are overcrowded, and traffic is severely congested, especially during rush hours. Noise and air pollution caused by traffic and factories affect the health of metropolitan residents. Population growth has led to a shortage of schools and hospitals, as well as to the problem of disposing of growing amounts of waste.

Tokyo is part of the Keihin Industrial Zone, which also includes the major industrial centers of Kawasaki (population 1.2 million) and Yokohama (population 3.3 million). Because Tokyo's port at the head of Tokyo Bay lacks a natural deepwater harbor, most of the cargo handled in the capital is carried by smaller, domestic ships. Yokohama, however, is located close to the mouth of the bay and serves as the nation's chief port for international trade. Yokohama is also Japan's second largest city.

Japan's third largest urban area is centered in Osaka (population 2.6 million) and includes Kyoto (population 1.5 million) and Kobe

Tokyo, Japan's capital city, has a population density of more than 1,000 people per square mile (386 people per sq. km). For a link to the most up-to-date population figures for Japan, go to vgsbooks.com.

(population 1.4 million). Located on Osaka Bay along the southern coast of Honshu, Osaka is a major industrial, financial, and commercial center, as well as the home of Japanese drama. Numerous canals and rivers crisscross the city, but in the 1960s city planners began to replace many of Osaka's waterways with roads and highways.

Not only a manufacturing city, Kyoto is also a center for Japanese art and religion. The capital of the Japanese imperial court for several centuries, Kyoto has also been called Heian-kyo ("Capital of Peace and Tranquility") and Miyako ("Imperial City"). Factories in Kyoto produce porcelain, lacquerware, brocades, and bronze statues, as well as electrical equipment, chemicals, and textiles.

Several other cities on Honshu support shipping and manufacturing industries. These include Hiroshima, Kure, and Okayama on the Inland Sea and Nagoya on Ise Bay. Nagoya is Japan's fourth largest urban area, with 2.1 million inhabitants.

Major cities on Kyushu include Fukuoka (population 1.3 million) and Kitakyushu (population 1 million). The largest population center on Shikoku is Matsuyama (population 461,000). Sapporo (population 1.8 million) is the largest commercial and manufacturing center on Hokkaido.

HISTORY AND GOVERNMENT

Archaeological finds suggest that humans inhabited the Japanese islands as long as 200,000 years ago. The people living in the region, however, did not keep historical records until the fifth century A.D.

According to Shinto myth (Shinto is the ancient religion of Japan), Jimmu Tenno founded the first Japanese state in 660 B.C. A legendary descendant of Amaterasu, the sun goddess, Jimmu is said to have begun an unbroken line of emperors that continues into the twenty-first century.

◉ Prehistory

The first identifiable culture in Japan is the Jomon civilization, which lasted from about 10,000 B.C. to 250 B.C. The people of this period lived in pit dwellings (houses whose main floors were slightly below ground level) and obtained food by hunting, gathering, and fishing. In the third century B.C., immigrants from China and Korea began to arrive

in Japan. This immigration marked the beginning of the Yayoi culture, which lasted until about A.D. 250.

In the second century B.C., new immigrants from the Asian continent brought bronze and iron tools with them to Japan. These settlers also introduced rice cultivation, which eventually became the mainstay of the Japanese farming economy.

Another Japanese civilization arose in the fourth century A.D. Centered on the fertile Yamato Plain east of present-day Osaka, the Yamato culture developed a centralized, clan-based empire. The powerful Yamato clan extended its authority to include a small coastal kingdom in southern Korea called Mimana, which lasted until A.D. 562. Also known as the age of the Kofun (great tomb mounds), the Yamato period saw the construction of earthen burial mounds for chieftains. Building these huge tombs required large-scale social and political organization. Enclosed in the tombs along with the dead were numerous artifacts, such as ornaments, tools, weapons, and clay statues called haniwa.

The door to a tomb lies almost unnoticed at the entrance to this great earthen burial mound, called a Kofun. The mound was most likely built between A.D. 300 and 710, during the Yamato period.

Chinese Influence

During the next several centuries, elements of Chinese civilization entered Japan from Korea, a region heavily influenced by Chinese culture. By the end of the fifth century A.D., the Japanese had adopted the Chinese system of writing and had adapted it to their own speech patterns. Confucianism—Chinese guidelines for correct personal behavior and good government—began to spread throughout Japan.

Buddhism, a religion that originated in India, also came to Japan from China and Korea. In the early 500s, Buddhist priests journeyed from Korea to Japan, bringing with them Buddhist images and scriptures, calendars, and methods of keeping time. In the seventh century, Buddhism became Japan's official religion and strongly influenced Shinto.

In 607 a mission sent by Prince Shotoku to China carried a letter to the Chinese emperor. This letter referred to Japan as the "land of the rising sun" for the first time in written history.

During this period, Japanese rulers began to model their government more closely after the centralized Chinese system. Prince Shotoku sent envoys to China to learn more about Chinese society. In 645 new leaders began the Taika Reform, introducing features of Chinese government that included the promotion of people through education and merit. New laws divided the country into administrative units, instituted a central system of taxation, and put in place a

In the seventh century A.D., Japan's imperial rulers decided they wanted to model Japan's society after China's. **Prince Shotoku** *(center)* of Japan sent envoys to neighboring China to study the way of life there.

land-distribution program. A capital was established at Nara in 710. In 794 the imperial government moved to Heian-kyo, a city that many Japanese simply called Kyoto ("Capital City"). Heian-kyo remained the center of power for the next four hundred years—a time known as the Heian period.

Fujiwara Leadership

During the early Heian period, the Fujiwara, an aristocratic family, gradually gained power over the emperor and his court by marrying members of the imperial family. Intent on maintaining their high position in Japanese society, the Fujiwara reversed many elements of the Taika Reform. These reforms had made efforts to reward people based upon their skills and abilities, but the Fujiwara won influence through family connections. By the mid-ninth century, the Fujiwara had gained mastery over Japan, and they held control for the next three centuries. Although the emperors still officially reigned, they had lost all real power.

Despite some social setbacks, the arts flowered during the Fujiwara period. The classical age of Japanese literature dates from the reign of

Michinaga (995–1027), the greatest Fujiwara leader. During this period, Lady Murasaki Shikibu wrote *The Tale of Genji*—one of the greatest works in all Japanese literature.

Because the Fujiwara had reversed many of the Taika Reforms, land became concentrated in the hands of court aristocrats and Buddhist monasteries. These landholdings grew to be privately controlled estates, or *shoen*. The estates were not taxed and did not come under the authority of government officials. Estate owners, called daimyo, became quite powerful and kept private bands of warriors, or samurai, to protect their land. Military

Lady Murasaki Shikibu

chieftains who led large groups of samurai gradually gained control of many estates and challenged the authority of the central government.

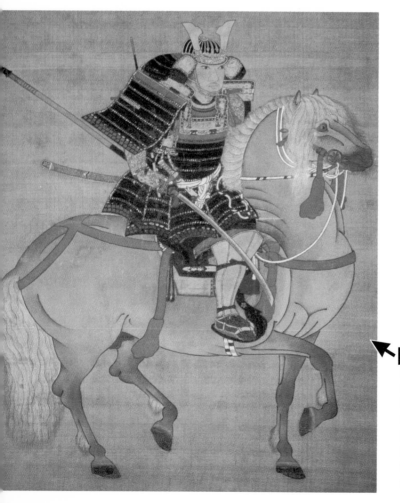

Samurai defended the interests of their lords— wealthy estate owners. Samurai were known for their fierce loyalty, self-discipline, honor, and bravery. In time samurai formed their own class within Japanese society.

Two of the most powerful bands of samurai were headed by the Taira and the Minamoto families, who fought against each other for control of the Heian court. The Taira seized control from the Fujiwara in 1160, but in 1180 the Minamoto began another civil war. After five years, the Minamoto defeated the Taira, and the warrior Yoritomo became the first Minamoto leader of Japan.

Kamakura Period

Establishing a military capital at Kamakura separate from the imperial seat in Heian-kyo, Yoritomo began a military dictatorship. This style of government remained in place in Japan for the next seven centuries. In 1192 the emperor named Yoritomo a shogun—a supreme military commander—and his government came to be known as a shogunate. Although the emperor retained his position, the shogun and the shogun's advisers exercised complete power.

After Yoritomo's death in 1199, control of the shogunate shifted to the Hojo, the family of Yoritomo's wife. Hojo power gradually weakened during the 1200s. Daimyo grew stronger and challenged the authority of the shogunate, which meanwhile was defending Japan against the invasions of Mongol troops from east central Asia.

The Ashikaga Shogunate

The Kamakura period ended in 1333, when the emperor Go-Daigo rebelled against Hojo rule. Aided by General Ashikaga Takauji, Go-Daigo overthrew the Hojos, but Takauji revolted and took power himself in 1338. He drove the emperor out of Kyoto and established the Ashikaga shogunate.

After their success in gaining power, Ashikaga rulers found themselves unable to control the daimyo and unite the country. Local wars between rival factions became so common that the period, which lasted until the mid-sixteenth century, is sometimes referred to as the Era of Warring States.

Despite political upheaval, Japanese culture continued to develop

DIVINE WINDS

In 1274 Kublai Khan, leader of the Mongol Empire, attacked the Japanese island of Kyushu with a large fleet of ships and thousands of soldiers. Japanese forces were no match for the invading army, but a sudden serious storm destroyed many of the enemy's ships and forced them to retreat. In 1281 Kublai Khan launched a second, larger attack, only to be thwarted again by an even more violent storm. The Japanese called these storms *kamikaze*, or "divine winds," a name that would later be applied to Japanese suicide pilots in World War II.

during the Ashikaga shogunate. The court supported the arts, and Buddhist monasteries served as centers of learning and art. New artistic forms arose, both Chinese influenced and solely Japanese in origin. Social barriers became less rigid, although the landless peasants were still at the bottom of the social hierarchy (social power structure).

Japan also prospered economically during this period. Agricultural methods improved, and foreign trade increased. Exports included fine crafts such as painted screens, folding fans, and ornate swords. More people began to use money instead of bartering to pay for purchases, and new commercial cities and market towns were built.

Portuguese traders reached Japan in the mid-sixteenth century. A Spanish Roman Catholic priest, Francis Xavier, landed at Kagoshima on southern Kyushu in 1549. He converted some Japanese to the Catholic religion, and missionaries and traders continued to arrive from Spain and Portugal. In the succeeding decades, traders also came from the Netherlands and England. The Europeans brought potatoes, tobacco, muskets, and gunpowder to Japan.

After centuries of internal conflict, Japan became more unified in the late 1500s. Powerful daimyo gained control over weaker ones, and in 1582, Toyotomi Hideyoshi, a skillful military commander, took power. Hideyoshi accomplished the unification of the main

The Portuguese arrive in Japan, bearing goods from Europe. In the sixteenth century, the Portuguese dominated world trade.

islands of Japan, although Hokkaido and the outlying Ryukyu and Bonin Islands were not officially incorporated into the country until the 1800s.

The 1600s to 1867

Tokugawa Ieyasu

Tokugawa Ieyasu succeeded Hideyoshi after the commander's death in 1598. In 1603 the emperor appointed Ieyasu shogun, and the new ruler established his headquarters in Edo (modern Tokyo). For the next 250 years, the Tokugawa shogunate reigned supreme.

Fearing that European conquerors would follow the Christian missionaries, Tokugawa shoguns cut off Japan's contact with the outside world. By the mid-seventeenth century, Japan had become an isolated country. The Tokugawa believed this isolation would enable them to maintain internal order, and Japan did enjoy a period of increased stability. But by the eighteenth century, changing social and economic conditions signaled the beginning of new directions in Japan. A large, wealthy merchant class gained great strength, and landless peasants seeking to improve their impoverished conditions rebelled. Japan renewed international relations when the Tokugawa shogunate relaxed its restrictions, especially in the areas of science, medicine, and languages.

The greatest force for change came from outside rather than from inside Japan. Russia, Great Britain, the United States, and France began to pressure the shogunate to open Japanese ports to foreign trade. These nations possessed advanced weapons, which made their demands hard to ignore. Japan was forced to reconsider its policy of seclusion.

In 1853 the U.S. government sent Commodore Matthew C. Perry to

In 1701 Asano Naganori, a Japanese estate owner, was condemned to death by suicide for drawing his sword in the home of the shogun. His samurai then became *ronin*, or masterless warriors. Forty-seven of these ronin plotted for two years before carrying out their plan to avenge Asano's death, upon which they themselves were condemned to suicide. Despite their fate, the forty-seven ronin were considered the most loyal and honorable of samurai, and their story is still a favorite among the Japanese as a tale of great heroism.

A scroll depicts the **arrival of Commodore Matthew C. Perry's fleet,** which was sent to Japan by the United States in 1853.

convince the Japanese emperor to open the country. Entering the bay at Edo with four warships, Perry demanded that Japan begin diplomatic and trade relations with the United States. Several months later, the Tokugawa government signed a treaty granting the United States its request.

Soon Great Britain, France, the Netherlands, and Russia also signed commercial treaties with Japan. These agreements gave the foreign powers rights that Japan did not receive in return, and internal enemies of the Tokugawa shogunate strongly criticized the government for signing such unequal treaties.

Daimyo from western Japan plotted to overthrow the shogunate and restore imperial power. In 1867 troops fighting for the daimyo forced the shogun to resign, and the emperor regained his traditional powers. The following year Japan's capital was moved from Kyoto to Edo, which was renamed Tokyo ("Eastern Capital").

The Meiji Restoration

The reigning emperor, Mutsuhito, adopted the name Meiji, meaning "enlightened rule," as his own title and as a name for the period, which lasted until his death in 1912. The emperor immediately announced his intention to modernize Japan, using European countries as a model. He sent Ito Hirobumi, a prominent political figure, to Europe to study systems of government. Japan's first constitution, enacted in 1889, protected imperial power but also created a two-house parliament, called the Diet. Ito was the nation's first prime minister.

Ito Hirobumi

Meiji leaders also greatly expanded the educational system and made schooling compulsory. They abolished the samurai class, replacing it with an army and a navy patterned after European examples. Transportation and communication systems were modernized, as were banking and taxation practices. Meiji leaders also encouraged industrialization by hiring U.S. and European experts in many fields. By the 1920s, *zaibatsu*—huge corporations owned by single families—controlled the economy.

Japanese Imperialism

Through its rapid modernization, Japan not only avoided European colonization but also transformed itself into a world power. By 1879 Japan had made the Ryukyu Islands an official part of its territory. Japan next turned its attention to Korea, which was under Chinese influence. When Japan urged China to recognize Korea's independence, tension mounted between China and Japan. In 1894 the Chinese-Japanese War broke out, and the Japanese forces defeated the Chinese. Under the Treaty of Shimonoseki, Japan gained Taiwan and the Penghus (Pescadores)—a group of islands between Taiwan and China. Korea maintained its independence.

Rivalry also developed between Japan and Russia over their conflicting interests in Korea and Manchuria, a Chinese region that Russia had occupied in 1900. After negotiation attempts between the two countries failed, Japan attacked a Russian fleet off the coast of southern Manchuria in 1904, touching off the Russo-Japanese War. The conflict was costly for both countries. Japan won its second modern war and added more lands to its territory under the Treaty of Portsmouth.

World War I and World War II

When World War I broke out in 1914, Japan sided with Great Britain against Germany, hoping to take over German holdings in eastern

Japanese soldiers stand with weapons carriers in World War I. As a result of the war, Japan gained territory and new economic markets, increasing its importance in Asia.

Asia. In 1919, at the postwar peace conference at Versailles, France, Japan was recognized as one of the world's major military and industrial powers.

After World War I, Japanese foreign policy focused on developing trade rather than expanding territory. As a member of the League of Nations—an organization dedicated to world peace—Japan supported many peace-seeking measures. During the 1920s, the Japanese parliamentary government became increasingly democratic as new political parties emerged and new election laws were enacted.

The worldwide economic depression of the 1930s, however, affected Japan's political development. A troubled economy, coupled with concern over China's reestablishment of control in Manchuria, enabled Japanese military leaders to gain increasing importance. They led the government away from democracy and toward totalitarianism, or rule by a dictator such as a military official. In 1931 the Japanese invaded Manchuria and set up the state of Manchukuo. They then extended their influence to other parts of northern China and threatened to occupy Chinese cities. When the League of Nations condemned Japan's actions, Japan withdrew from the organization.

Supported by the economically powerful zaibatsu, the military virtu-

In September 1923, the Great Kanto Earthquake struck Japan, devastating most of Yokohama and a large part of Tokyo. The quake itself and the widespread fires that followed left more than 100,000 people dead and some 3 million homeless. A hall in modern Tokyo stands in memory of the disaster's victims.

ally came to rule Japan. The Japanese Empire adopted a policy of aggressive expansion, and a clash between a Chinese patrol and Japanese troops near Beijing in 1937 flared into open warfare between the two countries. By the end of 1938, Japan controlled most of eastern China. The Japanese military began to speak of uniting all of eastern Asia under Japanese rule. Called the Greater East Asia Co-Prosperity Sphere, this proposed union was intended to free Asian areas from European colonization.

The beginning of World War II in Europe in September 1939 gave Japan another opportunity to expand its empire. A year later, Japan occupied the northern part of French Indochina (in Southeast Asia) and signed an agreement of alliance with Germany and Italy. When Japanese troops entered southern Indochina in 1941, the United States cut off exports to Japan. Later that year, General Tojo Hideki became prime minister of Japan, and military leaders began planning for war with the United States.

On December 7, 1941, Japanese bombers launched a surprise attack on the U.S. naval base at Pearl Harbor in Hawaii, as well as on U.S. bases on Guam and Wake Island in the Pacific. The next day, the United States and its European allies against Germany declared war on Japan. Gaining quick initial victories, Japan reached its greatest expansion in 1942.

U.S. military men at **Pearl Harbor** on Oahu, one of the Hawaiian Islands, watch in shock after the Japanese surprise attack on the U.S. naval base.

In June 1942, the tide of the war began to turn when the United States defeated Japan in the Battle of Midway in the central Pacific. As the number of Japanese defeats rose, political discontent within Japan grew. In 1944 Prime Minster Tojo and his cabinet were forced to resign.

Early in 1945, U.S. bombers and warships began to attack industrial and trade targets within Japan. On August 6, 1945, the United States targeted Hiroshima, an industrial city on southern Honshu, dropping the first atomic bomb ever used in warfare. On August 9, the United States dropped a second atomic bomb, striking Nagasaki on Kyushu.

Japan's emperor Hirohito agreed to a complete surrender on August 14. On September 2, a Japanese representative signed the formal surrender aboard the battleship USS *Missouri* in Tokyo Bay. Japan lost all the territory it had gained on the Asian mainland, as well as its Pacific holdings beyond the four main islands and the small islands nearby. Millions of people on both sides of the conflict had died during the war. Every major Japanese city except Kyoto had suffered heavy bombing, and the nation's economy was in ruins.

◉ Military Occupation

In late August 1945, Japan was placed under the military occupation of the Allied Powers (those countries that had fought against

Hiroshima lies in ruins after the devastating blast of the atomic bomb dropped on the city by U.S. forces in 1945. To learn more about the effects of the atomic bombs dropped on Hiroshima and Nagasaki, visit vgsbooks.com for links containing additional information and photographs.

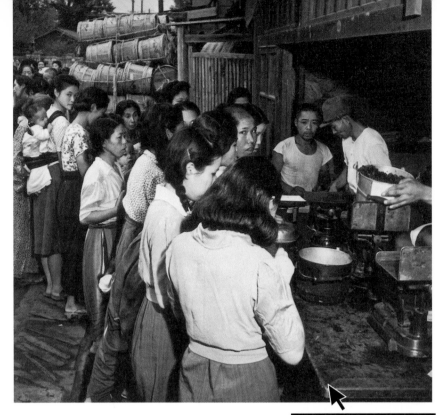

After World War II, many Japanese had to rely on food distribution centers for daily meals.

Germany, Italy, and Japan during World War II). The occupation forces sought to end Japanese militarism and to establish a democratic government in Japan. U.S. general Douglas MacArthur, the supreme commander for the Allied Powers in the Pacific, led the military's efforts.

MacArthur and his advisers drafted a new Japanese constitution, which went into effect in 1947. The document transferred political power from the emperor to the Japanese people, dissolved the army and navy, and forbade Japan to use war as a political weapon. Women gained the right to vote and were elected to the Diet.

MacArthur also began economic reforms, aided by financial support from the United States. A land-reform program enabled Japanese farmers to buy the land they worked rather than to rent it. New laws dissolved the powerful zaibatsu and established labor unions.

Until 1925 only men paying a certain amount in taxes had the right to vote in Japan. Voting rights were extended to all adult men in 1925 and to adult women in 1947.

By 1949 the major aims of the occupation had been achieved, and the Allied occupation officially ended in 1952. A 1951 security treaty between the United States and Japan permitted the United States to maintain military bases and troops in Japan.

Japan's economy recovered quickly after World War II. By the mid-1950s, industrial output equaled prewar levels. In 1966 **the automobile industry** in Japan produced more than 2 million four-door vehicles, making Japan the second-largest car manufacturer in the world.

Postwar Boom

After World War II, Japan swiftly rebuilt its economy and became a leader in world trade. Several factors contributed to Japan's rapid recovery. Investing heavily in new plants and equipment, the Japanese focused on products that could be traded on the world market. Because international trade grew rapidly after the war, Japan was able to import modern technology and raw materials at a relatively low cost and then to sell finished goods to foreign countries. As the improving economy brought increased wages, Japan's standard of living rose. The Japanese became more of a consumer society, and the nation's class structure loosened.

In 1955 members of competing political groups united to form the conservative Liberal Democratic Party (LDP), which held uninterrupted control over Japan's national government for thirty-eight years. The resulting political stability enabled long-term economic planning.

Despite successful domestic policies, unrest arose in Japan over the presence of U.S. troops. Riots broke out in 1960, when many Japanese protested the signing of the Treaty of Mutual Cooperation and Security with the United States. This document extended the 1951 security agreement between the two nations, continuing the presence of U.S. bases and troops in Japan.

In 1968 the United States returned the Bonin Islands to Japan, and in 1972, Japan regained complete control of the Ryukyus. Both island groups had been occupied by the United States after World War II. A dispute over

In June 1960, **30,000 demonstrators protested** at the U.S. Embassy in Tokyo. Many Japanese objected to the continued presence of U.S. troops in Japan.

the Russian-held Kuril Islands, four of which Japan claims, is still unresolved, despite meetings in 2001 between officials from both nations.

Troubled Economy

In the 1980s and 1990s, international trade imbalances threatened Japan's position in the world market. Tensions arose between Japan and its trading partners—particularly the United States—who complained that competition from Japanese industries was hurting the sale of their own products. Japanese trade barriers that limited imports into Japan also frustrated some foreign countries. They argued that Japan should strive to equalize its trade imbalance by buying more imports and selling fewer exports. In response to these criticisms, Japan began to limit some exports, such as automobiles, although Japan's powerful automotive industry still exports a large number of vehicles. U.S. and Japanese officials continued to discuss trade agreements during the 1990s, and by the end of the twentieth century Japan had loosened many of its old restrictions on imports.

Despite its strong international position as a manufacturer and exporter, Japan's economy suffered throughout the 1990s, as interest levels rose and prices fell. An economic recession set in that continues to plague the nation with rising levels of bankruptcy, unemployment, and homelessness. In addition to these economic concerns, Japan faced a series of political scandals in the 1990s. The large number of politicians, banking officials, and other public figures engaged in corrupt activities, combined with the lenient treatment of many of the offenders, led to public outrage and demands for reform. In 1993 a coalition of seven small political parties acquired enough seats to form a new government with the goal of reform. For the first time in thirty-eight years, the LDP was not in charge of the Japanese government. Following this upheaval, continued political instability brought seven different prime ministers to power over a period of eight years.

Two domestic crises shook Japan further in 1995, beginning with the Great Hanshin Earthquake, which hit Kobe in January, killing more than six thousand people and destroying thousands of homes. In March of the same year, a Japanese religious sect released a poisonous gas into Tokyo's subway system, killing twelve people and injuring thousands more. In November of 1995, public dissatisfaction with U.S. military bases and personnel in Japan, especially in Okinawa, resurfaced as a major issue. In 1996 an agreement between the United States and Japan called for a portion of the land occupied by U.S. military sites to be returned gradually to Japanese control.

On the political scene, the LDP regained control of the government in 1996, but Japan's struggling economy led to worries and uncertainty as the nation faced the twenty-first century. In 2001 the Bank of Japan cut interest rates and the government announced budget cuts in an effort to improve the country's financial situation. Despite these measures, a plummeting stock market, deflation (falling prices of goods and land), and continued government debt put Prime Minister Yoshiro Mori under pressure to resign. In April 2001, Koizumi Junichiro was sworn in as Japan's prime minister. Even as the new

Smoke fills the sky from fires caused by the **Great Hanshin Earthquake** of 1995. More than six thousand lives were lost in the earthquake.

leader took office, the Japanese government continued to face ongoing domestic challenges. Housing shortages, widespread pollution, and a growing percentage of elderly Japanese are all issues that leaders must address to meet the changing needs of the Japanese people.

On the political scene, the LDP regained control of the government in 1996, but Japan's struggling economy led to uncertainty as the nation faced the beginning of the twenty-first century. In April 2001, Koizumi Junichiro was sworn in as Japan's new prime minister. That same year, the Bank of Japan cut interest rates, and the government announced budget cuts to improve the country's financial situation. Despite these measures, Japan was facing a looming bank crisis by 2002 due to factors including a plummeting stock market, deflation (falling prices of goods and land), continued government debt, and billions of dollars in unpaid loans. The Japanese government also faces ongoing domestic challenges. Housing shortages, widespread pollution, and a growing percentage of elderly Japanese are all issues that leaders must address to meet the changing needs of the Japanese people.

▷ Government

The Constitution of 1947 made Japan a democratic state. Power is vested in the Japanese people, while the emperor is the ceremonial and symbolic head of the nation. The throne is inherited by male descendants of the imperial family. Japan's constitution guarantees many human liberties, such as freedom of speech, of religion, of the press, and of assembly. Three branches—executive, legislative, and judicial—make up the government.

Executive power is held by a cabinet, which is headed by a prime minister. The Diet, Japan's legislative body, names the prime minister, who is usually the leader of the political party that has the most seats in the legislature. The prime minister chooses the cabinet ministers, the majority of whom must be from the Diet. All cabinet members must be civilians, and they are responsible to the Diet. The Japanese people elect upper-house members of the Diet every six years and lower-house representatives every four years.

The nation's judicial system has several levels. At the top is a supreme court, headed by a chief justice, with fourteen associate justices. The cabinet selects supreme court members. Below this body are regional high courts, district courts, family courts, and summary courts. Family courts handle all domestic cases, and summary courts hear cases involving minor offenses and small claims.

For administrative purposes, Japan is divided into forty-seven prefectures. Voters in each prefecture elect a governor and an assembly every four years. The local regions are further divided into cities, towns, and villages, each of which has its own elected mayor and assembly.

THE PEOPLE

With 127 million people, Japan is one of the world's most heavily populated countries. The population density averages about 870 people per square mile (336 people per sq. km), compared to 74 (29 per sq. km) in the United States and 342 (132 per sq. km) in China, but it is much higher in some parts of the nation. About 90 percent of all Japanese live on the coastal plains, which cover less than one-quarter of the country's landmass. In Tokyo, an average of over 30,000 people are crowded into each square mile (over 11,583 people per sq. km). Over three-quarters of the population live in urban areas, but overcrowding and the high cost of living in Japan's largest cities have led many people to begin settling in smaller, regional cities.

◉ Ethnic Background

Primarily of Mongolian background, most Japanese are descended from various peoples who migrated to the islands from the northeast-

ern part of the Asian mainland. Some Japanese ancestors may also have come from islands south of Japan. Because Japan has a history free of foreign invasions, scientists believe that the language and appearance of the modern Japanese people have changed little since the days of the Yayoi culture (250 B.C. to A.D. 250). Traditionally, very few Japanese marry foreigners.

The Japanese exhibit a strong national pride and national identity. Furthermore, Japanese society is structured to encourage people to identify with and to conform to a group, such as the family, the school, or the corporation. Social events and group activities are an important part of strengthening this shared sense of community.

MINORITIES A small number of minorities exist in Japan. The largest of these—the approximately two million *burakumin*, or out-casts—is actually culturally and ethnically Japanese. Nevertheless, these people face greater discrimination than any other group in Japan because they or their ancestors have been associated with occupations that involve blood and death. These activities—which include butchering, tanning, and shoemaking—are considered unclean, and people who engage in them are thought to be contaminated. Historically, burakumin were forced to live apart from the rest of the population in villages or settlements called *buraku.* Although their segregation is no longer enforced by the government, many burakumin have difficulty obtaining adequate housing, education, and employment. Groups such as the Buraku Liberation League have been established to seek greater rights for burakumin, but their situation has improved little.

The second largest minority group in Japan is of Korean descent. The ancestors of some of these people immigrated to Japan as long ago as the sixteenth century. Others arrived between 1930 and 1945 to fill Japanese industry's growing need for labor. Many of these Korean immigrants were pressured to change their names to sound more Japanese. The Korean community numbers over 600,000. Its members, who are rarely granted Japanese citizenship, face discrimination in education, in social interaction, and in employment.

A third minority group is the Ainu, whose ancestors may have been the first inhabitants of Japan. Some scholars believe the Ainu are

The **Ainu practice a traditional dance.** Many experts consider the Ainu to be the first inhabitants of Japan. The Ainu have kept many of their traditions alive for centuries.

related to European peoples. Others think they are descended from Asians or from the original inhabitants of Australia. People of Ainu descent, who look unlike other Japanese, number about 15,000. The Ainu language, which is distinct from Japanese and has no written form, is no longer in common conversational use but is preserved in an oral tradition of stories and songs. The Ainu inhabit a small area on Hokkaido, where they have lived for centuries after having been pushed northward to harsher climates by the expanding Japanese population. Historically victims of discrimination, the Ainu have begun a movement to gain fair treatment, and the Japanese government has granted them some economic aid.

There is also a small population of foreigners living and working in Japan. Although Japan's ongoing need for labor allows these people to reside in Japan temporarily, many foreigners face some resistance to their presence. Japanese citizens who live abroad and return to Japan often face similar challenges in gaining acceptance.

Language

Language experts consider Japanese one of the world's most difficult languages to learn. Some scholars have argued that it is unrelated to any other language, while others say that it belongs to the Altaic group, which includes Korean, Finnish, Hungarian, and Turkish. Japanese has words from European, Chinese, and Indian sources and employs an adapted version of the Chinese system of writing. The unique language resulting from this blend has been almost entirely confined to the Japanese islands, contributing both to the unity of the Japanese people and to their cultural isolation from the rest of the world.

One of the characteristics of Japanese that makes it such a difficult language to master is its use of special forms of speech to convey

Japanese characters on lanterns

Many dialects, or regional variations, of the Japanese language exist. Some of these dialects are so different from each other that speakers from certain areas of Japan are unable to understand those from other areas. However, the Tokyo dialect is most commonly used in newspapers, radio broadcasts, and TV programs, and most Japanese can communicate using this dialect.

differences in status between speakers. People must consider whether the person they are talking to is of superior or inferior position and whether the person is a new acquaintance or an intimate member of their own group. Different verb forms indicate these various relationships between speakers. Men and women also speak differently from each other, even using separate vocabularies. Furthermore, a very complex system of symbols makes written Japanese extremely difficult even for native speakers to master.

Social Structure

The system of social class and rank in Japan became less rigid in the twentieth century. However, attitudes and ideas regarding social status are still evident, and specific rules of behavior continue to govern interaction among people of various social positions.

An individual's status in Japan is determined primarily by his or her age and gender. Other factors, such as education and employment, may also play a role. An older person is always considered superior to a younger person, no matter how small the age difference, and males are ranked higher than females. Although the status of Japanese women has improved since World War II, treatment of the sexes remains unequal. For example, language and customs are slowly developing that acknowledge the presence of women in a previously all-male workplace, but working women still face major challenges such as unequal pay and slower advancement.

Regardless of personal status, the group is always valued more highly by Japanese society than any individual. The family, community, nation, company, and school class are considered very important. From childhood, individuals are expected to suppress traits or desires that conflict with those of the group.

As a result of this emphasis on the group's success, the Japanese spend much time and effort maintaining harmony within and among groups. The *nakodo*, or go-between, plays a central role in intergroup relations, beginning almost any interaction between people. Introductions made by the nakodo are crucial to successful negotia-

Employees gather at a company picnic during the Cherry Blossom Festival. Building team spirit is part of the Japanese cultural emphasis on community.

tions in social and business arrangements, and elaborate social courtesies guide most social contact.

Harmony is also achieved by making each person feel like an important member of the group. Decisions are made only after consulting everyone in the group. Extra social activities strengthen group spirit further. For example, employees build closeness by participating in regular activities outside of work, such as meeting in a restaurant at the end of the day.

In addition to maintaining strong groups, the Japanese strive continually to improve themselves as individuals. Self-improvement is demonstrated in relationships with other people, the mastery of arts and sports, and a strong work ethic. The Japanese believe that labor is essential to personal growth and that people must be prepared to endure long periods of unrewarded work before they achieve success. Traits such as inner strength and discipline are admired and contribute to these attitudes toward personal development.

BOWING TO ETIQUETTE

An important part of Japanese social interaction is the bow as a form of greeting, thanks, apology, and more. Just as verbal greetings differ according to status, so do bows. In general, the person of inferior rank is expected to bow lower and for a longer period of time than the superior party. What should you do when visiting a Japanese home? To find out, go to vgsbooks.com for links regarding etiquette in Japan.

Marriage and Family

The institution of family is important to Japanese culture, and many traditional customs regarding marriage and children are still valued and observed. Japan's divorce rate remains low compared to that of other industrial nations. Arranged marriages, although declining in number, are still more common in Japan than in most nations. Even marriages that are not formally arranged often make use of a nakodo. The go-between checks each party's background, conveys questions and criticisms, smooths out difficulties, and concludes the terms of the marriage agreement between the two families.

Traditional parenting roles in Japan assign the mother the part of primary caregiver and nurturer. Most Japanese fathers see their families little during the workweek but make a point to spend time with them on the weekends. While approximately half of all Japanese women join the workforce, many of them leave their jobs, at least temporarily, when they get married or have children. Japanese families have been shrinking since the late 1950s, with most modern couples having only one or two children. Many households still include grandparents and other members of the extended family, but this age-old practice is not as common as it was in the past.

A family meal in this household includes three generations. Although less common than in the past, some extended families still live together in Japan.

Students gather outside of class. The Japanese place an extremely high importance on education.

Education

Nine years of schooling—at the elementary and junior-high levels—are required of all Japanese children from the ages of 6 to 14. During these years, public education is free, and almost all children complete the requirements. In addition to studying traditional subjects such as math, science, and art, students spend a lot of time learning to read and write Japanese because the written language is so difficult. In junior high, most students also study English. Japan has a national literacy rate of about 99 percent.

Students who want to go on to senior high school must pass an entrance examination. About 95 percent of all junior-high graduates attend the three-year senior-high program, which prepares them for college or trains them for jobs. Most high schools have highly successful job placement programs to assist students. To enter a college or university, senior-high graduates must pass difficult entrance examinations. Competition for admission to the top institutions is intense, and special study schools exist to help applicants

Japanese students are under pressure to earn good grades and to pass the difficult entrance examinations for admission to secondary schools and universities. As a result, many students attend *juku*, or "cram schools," after school and on weekends. Some juku offer extra instruction in certain subjects, while others prepare students for general entrance exams.

In addition to regular class time, some **students attend "cram school"** to prepare for high-school and university entrance exams.

prepare for these exams. About one-third of all senior-high graduates enter a postsecondary school.

Japan has more than 1,000 junior colleges, colleges, and universities, the largest of which is Nihon University in Tokyo, with an enrollment of more than 80,000 students. There are also a number of government-funded national universities, including the University of Tokyo and Kyoto University, which have excellent reputations and are considered highly prestigious.

Health

With an average life span of 80 years, the Japanese are among the healthiest people in the world. During the last 55 years, the number of infants who died in their first year of life decreased from 60 for each 1,000 live births to fewer than 4 per 1,000. Cases of contagious diseases, such as tuberculosis and pneumonia, have also declined.

Better health statistics reflect overall improvements in general nutrition, in medical care, and in health insurance coverage. But new ailments—such as heart disease, cancer, and stroke—have replaced older afflictions and are due in part to dietary changes. As Japanese diets have become more like those of Europe and North America, with greater consumption of meat and dairy products, Japan's health problems have also become more like those of industrialized nations. Industrial pollution threatens the health of urban residents. Japan's intense business environment and its competitive role as a world economic leader have also led to high stress levels for many Japanese workers.

Care of the elderly is a growing concern in Japan, due to the rising percentage of elderly people in the population.

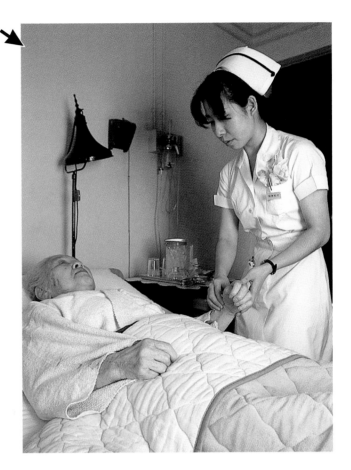

While life expectancy in Japan has increased, the birthrate has decreased. Consequently, the Japanese are anticipating a shortage of medical personnel to care for the growing percentage of elderly. This situation will pose one of the greatest challenges to Japanese medical services during the decades to come.

Japan has experienced a revival of traditional medicine in recent years as the world medical community has become interested in

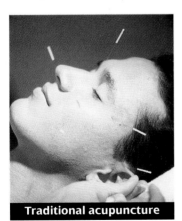

Traditional acupuncture

ancient Asian techniques. Much of traditional Japanese medicine stems from Chinese practices, such as herbal treatments and massage, but Japanese healers have contributed their own methods and variations. One of the most well known Asian medical procedures is acupuncture. An acupuncturist inserts very thin needles into various points on the patient's body to relieve pain and to cure disease. Since the 1950s, acupuncture has also been used to numb patients before and during surgery.

CULTURAL LIFE

With a cultural history spanning thousands of years, Japan's many arts, pastimes, and other expressions of culture have been highly refined and specialized. Yet despite their regard for tradition, the Japanese continue to expand and reshape their ideas and aesthetics. New forms, styles, and beliefs are constantly emerging, often influenced by aspects of other cultures as well as by Japan's own rich heritage.

▷ Religion

When compared with the people of many other Asian countries, the Japanese are strikingly secular (nonreligious). The residents of urban areas, in particular, seem indifferent to religious beliefs. This attitude has in part been shaped by Confucianism, a Chinese philosophy that sets forth ethical guidelines for behavior and which assumes that there are no supernatural beings to influence good conduct.

Nevertheless, most Japanese continue to participate in some religious observances. These occasions provide an opportunity for group

social activities, which are highly valued in Japanese society. The Japanese have adapted elements of various belief systems, including Shinto, Buddhism, and Christianity, to fit their society. In fact, many Japanese follow both Shinto and Buddhism.

Shinto, which means "the way of the gods," is Japan's oldest religion, dating from prehistoric times. Shintoists worship many gods, called *kami,* which are found in mountains, rivers, rocks, trees, and other parts of nature. Shintoists also worship the spirits of their ancestors. Buddhism, Japan's other main religion, arrived from China and Korea in the mid-sixth century A.D. and spread alongside Shinto. In general, Buddhists believe that peace and happiness can be achieved by renouncing one's attachment to worldly things and by leading a life of virtue and wisdom.

Beginning in the late nineteenth century, new religious groups began to form. These groups generally define themselves as either Shinto or Buddhist, depending on which religion contributes the most

New Year's Day draws many worshipers to a **Shinto shrine** in Kyoto. Many Japanese combine elements of both the Shinto and Buddhist religions. For links to up-to-date statistics, current events, and cultural data—including more on food, festivals, and religion—visit vgsbooks.com.

to their philosophy. The largest of the new religions is Soka Gakkai, a Buddhist sect.

Holidays and Festivals

The Japanese observe about a dozen national holidays, including Constitution Day and Children's Day. Most businesses and schools are closed on these days, and parades or fireworks may take place. Important events in the imperial family are also celebrated, such as royal weddings, the enthronement of new emperors, and the Emperor's Birthday.

Throughout the year, many festivals also take place around Japan. Most of these events are based on Shinto or Buddhism and may involve traditional ceremonies, but for many people, the modern purpose of these festivals is primarily social. Celebrations such as Obon (the Buddhist festival of the dead), Gion Matsuri (Kyoto's largest local celebration), and Sakura Matsuri (Cherry Blossom Festival) are good times for family and friends to gather and enjoy diversions, from folk dancing to picnics.

New Year's Day, or Oshogatsu, is the country's largest and most important celebration. New Year's is both a national holiday and an ancient festival, and observances during the season include visiting temples and shrines, attending parties, putting up household decorations, exchanging gifts, playing games, and enjoying a variety of special foods. Many of the traditions associated with Oshogatsu are intended to ensure good luck and a prosperous coming year.

Children march in a parade of the Nebuta Festival in Aomori. The festival is a purification ceremony. In earlier times, paper lanterns were floated out to sea, carrying away evil spirits. These days huge floats parade down the street.

Literature

Among the earliest written works in Japan are collections of poetry. One of the first significant contributions to Japanese literature was the *Man'yoshu*, an eighth-century anthology of more than four thousand poems. Japanese poems typically have subtle rhythms and no rhyme, and a fixed number of syllables determines the structure. The earliest poems, called tanka, deal with friendship, love, and nature. After the early fourteenth century, poets also composed *renga*, chains of linked verses written by several poets. The form of haiku developed during the Tokugawa period. Matsuo Basho (1644–1694) transformed haiku from a comic style into a serious art form that is still popular in Japan.

The Tale of Genji by Lady Murasaki Shikibu (ca. 978–ca. 1026) is generally considered one of the world's first novels and the greatest work of Japanese fiction. A detailed picture of tenth-century Heian court life, the work traces the adventures and loves of Prince Genji. During the civil wars of the thirteenth century, military epics such as *The Tale of the Heike* became popular.

In 1868 the Meiji Restoration marked the beginning of European influence on Japanese literature. Authors such as Futabatei Shimei and Tsubouchi Shoyo encouraged the Japanese to write novels that reflected Japan's new industrialization. Other novelists of the era include Natsume Soseki and Shiga Naoya. After World War II, popular, mass-market literature grew to attract readers from all parts of Japanese society.

Some modern writers have urged the Japanese to return to their traditional culture. One of the most famous of these authors is Mishima Yukio, whose reverence for the samurai tradition was so strong that he committed hara-kiri, killing himself in the ritual manner of a samurai. Nobel Prize winner Kawabata Yasunari also revered Japan's traditions, while other authors, such as Abe Kobo and Oe Kenzaburo, have examined modern Japanese society in the latter half of the twentieth century.

Drama and Music

Drama has been written and performed in Japan since the seventh century A.D. Since then it has evolved into a variety of forms that combine dramatic, musical, and dance elements. Japan's main theatrical styles are Noh, Bunraku, and Kabuki.

Noh plays are serious retellings of history and legend. Actors in Noh dramas wear painted wooden masks and reveal the play's story through carefully controlled gestures and movements. A chorus chants the lines of the play, and the sets and props are minimal. Because of the somber nature of Noh, light, humorous sketches called *kyogen* are often performed between Noh plays.

In Bunraku, a narrator recites the story to musical accompaniment. The plot is acted out by large, lifelike puppets, each requiring three people to manipulate it. Chikamatsu Monzaemon, Japan's greatest playwright, wrote several Bunraku masterpieces. Kabuki plays are melodramatic representations of historical or domestic events. Kabuki features colorful costumes and makeup, special effects, elaborate sets that may involve moving platforms and a revolving stage, and a lively, exaggerated acting style.

A musician plays the giant *taiko* drum at a festival of the vernal (spring) equinox. A skilled taiko artist can use the drum to produce sounds of gentle rain or the powerful winds of a typhoon.

Kabuki theater involves elaborate costumes, dramatic set design, and expressive makeup.

Traditional Japanese music, or *hogaku*, is still heard in modern Japan as an accompaniment to classical forms of drama and at festivals. Instruments used in hogaku include the *shamisen*, a three-stringed lute, the koto, or Japanese harp, *taiko* and *tsuzumi* drums, and the *shakuhachi*, a bamboo flute. *Kayokyoku*, or popular Japanese music, draws many listeners with concerts and television programs. Some musicians from Europe and North America have also gained a following in Japan.

For music lovers who like to join in, karaoke has been a popular activity in Japan since the 1980s. Dozens of karaoke bars allow participants to perform the vocals of well-known songs to the accompaniment of the taped instrumental portions. These establishments are favorite gathering places for businesspeople and students.

◎ Visual Arts and Multimedia

Although Chinese styles have strongly influenced Japanese art, the Japanese have adapted Chinese ideas to form their own tradition. Japanese artists have carefully used asymmetry and scaled-down subjects in their compositions. These techniques are evident in miniature rock gardens, bonsai (the art of cultivating dwarfed trees), and ikebana (flower arranging), artistic forms that have been a part of Japanese culture for more than one thousand years.

Japanese painting displays a great deal of attention to detail and often only hints at an

A Japanese artist creates a **flower arrangement** in competition. Ikebana, or flower arranging, is a traditional form of art practiced in Japan.

image or idea, leaving interpretation up to the viewer. The earliest Japanese paintings portray simple subjects related to the Buddhist faith, such as figures in meditation or scenes of nature. During the thirteenth and fourteenth centuries, artists painted long scrolls that depicted historical legends and other stories. Colorful wood-block prints, or ukiyo-e, were first created during the Tokugawa period and remain a popular art form. One of the most famous wood-block artists was Hokusai, whose series *Thirty-Six Views of Mount Fuji* depicts Japan's famous peak from many perspectives.

Calligraphy is another important art form in Japan. The nature of the written Japanese language allows skilled calligraphers to vary the shapes and styles of characters to evoke certain moods and to suggest different images and meanings.

Ukiyo-e, which means "pictures of the floating world," first floated to Europe in the mid-1800s. Packagers shipping Japanese goods to Europe used wood-block prints as wrapping paper.

In the mid-twentieth century, Japan became one of the world's leading producers of motion pictures. One of the most famous Japanese movies is *The Seven Samurai*, directed by Kurosawa Akira. In addition to providing entertainment, Japanese filmmakers have used their medium to examine Japanese history, traditions, and social issues.

Anime, or Japanese animation, has a wide audience in Japan and around the world. Originating in the 1960s, the first anime creations were intended for children. However, newer anime films and television programs are made for children and adults alike and cover themes from sports to horror stories.

Japanese comic books and comic strips, or *manga,* draw on a long history of caricature in Japanese art. Like anime, manga publications have many subjects and are popular with people of all ages. The popularity of manga and anime has contributed to the success of video games, which Japanese of all ages enjoy at home and in arcades. Another popular pastime is *pachinko,* an arcade game similar to pinball.

◉ Sports

Athletic activities in Japan range from traditional exercises to modern pastimes, some of which have been adopted from other countries. Sumo, a Japanese form of wrestling that is about two thousand years old, still draws huge crowds of spectators. The wrestlers themselves are huge, too—often over 6 feet (1.8 m) tall and weighing more than 250 pounds (114 kilograms). Sumo tournaments are highly ritualized and include preliminary rites to purify the wrestlers, to focus their strength, and to ensure the fairness of the match. The actual fight is fierce but brief, rarely lasting more than thirty seconds.

Many traditional forms of martial arts, such as judo, kendo, karate, and aikido, are popular in modern Japan. Judo, or "the way of softness," is a means of self-defense that does not result in bloodshed. Like other martial arts, judo was popular among samurai.

Baseball—one of the most popular sports in modern-day Japan—is of American origin. Many schools and companies have amateur teams, and some professional Japanese players, such as Suzuki Ichiro of the Seattle Mariners, have joined U.S. teams.

Two sumo wrestlers face off against each other in front of a crowd of thousands.

Golf is one of the most expensive sports in Japan, since the space needed for a golf course is rare in this crowded, mountainous country. Although fees for private clubs dropped toward the end of the 1990s, most memberships still cost thousands of dollars per year. Companies rather than individuals commonly pay the bill, as golf remains an extremely important means of establishing business contacts. Other popular sports in Japan include tennis, skiing, and ice skating, and Japan usually has strong Olympic teams in gymnastics, diving, and women's volleyball.

◉ Food and Dress

Like many other aspects of Japanese culture, daily necessities such as food and clothing have been modernized to some degree but still draw heavily on long traditions and customs. Japanese cuisine is known for its freshness, its simplicity, and its careful preparation. Rice and noodles form a part of nearly every meal. Tea is drunk at any time of the day, and sake, or rice wine, is a traditional favorite. Although European and North American influences have increased the proportion of meat and dairy products in the Japanese diet, seafood (including sushi and sashimi, which are prepared with seasoned rice and high-quality raw

JAPANESE NOODLES

In Japan, noodle shops serve up hot, delicious noodles to hungry customers all day long. To make them yourself, look for Japanese noodles and *dashinomoto* (powdered soup base) in the international foods section of your grocery store or at an Asian market.

6 c. water	4 tbsp. soy sauce
8 oz. soba, somen, or udon noodles	1 tbsp. sugar
3 c. water	chopped green onions or dried red pepper flakes
1 tbsp. dashinomoto	

1. Bring 6 cups of water to a boil. Add noodles and cook, stirring occasionally, for 20 minutes, or until noodles are soft.
2. Drain noodles in a colander and rinse in cool water. Divide noodles among four bowls.
3. In a saucepan, combine 3 cups water, dashinomoto, soy sauce, and sugar and bring to a boil. Remove from heat and pour broth over noodles. Top with chopped green onion or dried red pepper flakes and serve. Serves 4.

fish), fresh vegetables, and soybean products such as tofu and soy sauce are still primary ingredients. When preparing a meal, Japanese cooks are careful to serve combinations of dishes that provide both variety and harmony. They also make a great effort to present the food in a visually appealing manner.

In recent years, fast-food chains have become a common sight in large Japanese cities. Despite this trend, traditional noodle shops, sushi bars, and other Japanese restaurants all remain very popular places to meet and to dine.

Japanese dress has changed more drastically in modern times than Japanese cuisine has. Very few people in Japan wear traditional kimono, sandals, and other accessories on a daily basis. Most Japanese businesspeople wear suits to the office. Slacks, skirts, and shirts are the norm outside of work.

For special occasions, festival events, and holidays, many Japanese still don traditional clothing. Different styles of kimono may be worn according to the formality of the occasion and the age or marital status of the wearer. In addition to the kimono, men usually wear a loose coat bearing their family crest. While all kimono are similar in their basic shape, different ways of tying the obi (sash), the use of different fabrics, and the choice of footwear allow the expression of personal tastes.

A woman prepares tea for the *chanoyu*, or tea ceremony.

THE WAY OF TEA

The Japanese tea ceremony, a tradition hundreds of years old, is more than your average tea party. Its true focus is on serenity, respect, and beauty. In this highly ritualized ceremony, the host invites his or her guests to enter the tea room and admire a few decorations. The host then prepares and serves bowls of a special kind of powdered green tea, usually with a small sweet snack. The guests slowly drink their tea and enjoy the simple tranquility of the moment. For links to see how the tea room is set up and how the tea is prepared, visit vgsbooks.com.

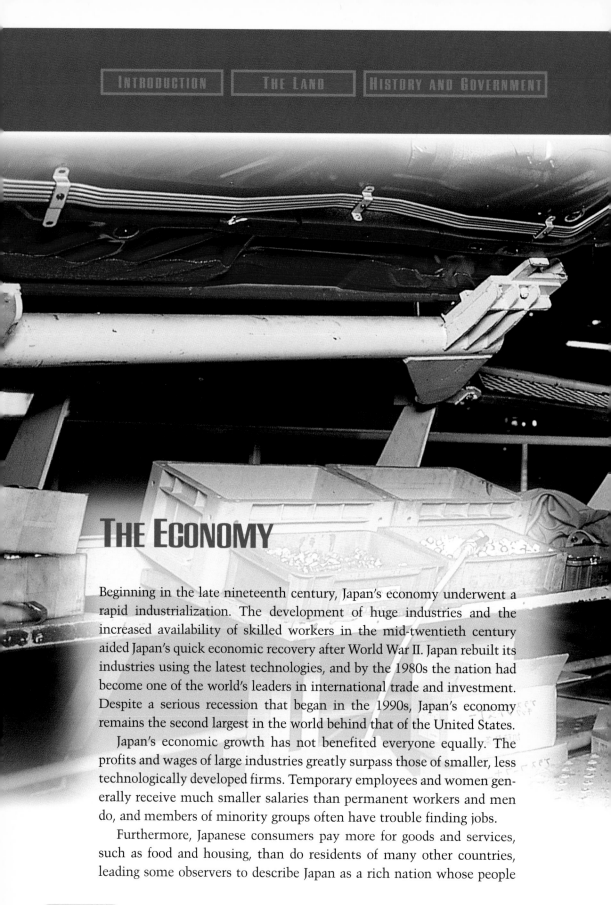

THE ECONOMY

Beginning in the late nineteenth century, Japan's economy underwent a rapid industrialization. The development of huge industries and the increased availability of skilled workers in the mid-twentieth century aided Japan's quick economic recovery after World War II. Japan rebuilt its industries using the latest technologies, and by the 1980s the nation had become one of the world's leaders in international trade and investment. Despite a serious recession that began in the 1990s, Japan's economy remains the second largest in the world behind that of the United States.

Japan's economic growth has not benefited everyone equally. The profits and wages of large industries greatly surpass those of smaller, less technologically developed firms. Temporary employees and women generally receive much smaller salaries than permanent workers and men do, and members of minority groups often have trouble finding jobs.

Furthermore, Japanese consumers pay more for goods and services, such as food and housing, than do residents of many other countries, leading some observers to describe Japan as a rich nation whose people are relatively poor. Despite this situation, very few people in Japan live in poverty. Although the Japanese pay more for items than they would in other countries, they still manage to save more money than do people elsewhere because they tend not to buy as much. Consequently, Japan imports far fewer goods than other countries, while it exports more than other countries. This has created a trade imbalance that has drawn complaints from Japan's trading partners. To level out this imbalance, Japanese officials have encouraged the nation's people to buy more consumer goods, and representatives of the government have met with foreign officials to consider trade agreements.

◉ Manufacturing

Japan's lack of significant natural resources has forced industrial development to depend on raw materials imported from other countries. Although Japanese industries are privately owned rather than state operated, government support of manufacturing has been crucial to

Japan's industrialization. Since World War II, the government has provided industry with low-interest loans and other economic assistance. In the late 1990s, manufacturing accounted for 23 percent of Japan's gross domestic product (the value of goods and services produced in Japan each year) and employed 21 percent of the nation's workforce.

Although Japan once had a reputation for making inexpensive, mass-produced goods, the Japanese have since developed some of the world's most advanced commercial technologies and business strategies. Manufacturers invest in the latest equipment and processes, making production less expensive and more efficient. This practice has lowered the price of Japanese exports, making them more competitive on the world market, and has also raised the quality of Japanese goods.

Japan, one of the world's leaders in shipbuilding, is also among the largest makers of electrical and electronic equipment, steel, and motor

Japan's ports bustle with activity, as imports and exports flow in and out of the country.

vehicles. Although the greatest emphasis is placed on industries that produce chemicals, petrochemicals, and heavy machinery, light industry also thrives. These factories produce radios, televisions, compact disc players, cameras, and computers. Japan was also once a leading supplier of silk. Textiles remain an important industry, although Japan's production of natural fibers such as silk and cotton has decreased while the production of synthetic materials has increased.

Japanese manufacturers continue to investigate the opportunities for new types of products. In the 1980s, Japan was well known for its production of entertainment-related products such as televisions, stereos, and VCRs. In recent years, the field of communications and information technology (IT), which includes pagers, electronic organizers, cellular phones, and Internet-related products, has found a growing market in Japan, especially among young people.

Despite the limited amount of space in most Japanese homes, the number of personal computers in Japan rose through the end of the twentieth century. Nonetheless, Internet use among the Japanese remains relatively low because of the high cost of phone lines. Japan's heavily populated cities and rugged rural terrain make phone lines expensive to install, and many people use portable cell phones in place of hardwired phones. As a result, wireless Internet connections through cell phones are popular, allowing users to

Cell phones are popular in Japan. Technologically advanced cell-phone users use their cell phones for everything from shopping to e-mail.

One of Japan's most high-tech manufacturing areas is robotics. Robots have been used in Japanese factories for decades, and modern researchers are also investigating the application of robotics to fields like construction and agriculture. By the beginning of the twenty-first century, toys such as robotic "pets"—including dogs, cats, and fish—had become very popular in Japan.

send e-mail, obtain news and other information, and shop on-line—a practice sometimes called e-commerce—without using permanent phone lines. By 1999 Japan had 48.5 million mobile-phone users, many of whom also used their phones to access the Internet.

The Japanese government has supported the information technology trend and has taken steps to ensure its continued success. In 2001 the government enacted a bill with the major goals of encouraging Internet use and providing computer education for Japanese students and adults.

Foreign Trade

One of the world's leading trading nations, Japan depends on its foreign commerce. This exchange is essential partly because the nation produces more than it consumes and partly because Japanese industries depend on imported raw materials.

To help keep the value of its exports higher than the value of its imports, Japan instituted trade barriers, such as taxes and quotas, to limit the number of incoming goods. This practice angered some of Japan's trading partners. In the mid-1980s, to maintain good international relations, Japan began to limit its exports, to relax some restrictions on imports, and to channel some of its huge trade surpluses to developing countries. It also began to build its own factories overseas to lessen the demand for products manufactured within Japan. Negotiations with major trading partners, particularly the United States and Asian nations such as China, continue into the twenty-first century.

Japan's most important exports are machinery (including automobiles), iron and steel, chemicals, and electronic equipment. Other major exports include plastics, ships, and synthetic fabrics. Japan imports petroleum, raw materials such as chemicals, coal, iron ore, natural gas, and timber, and food products such as meat and grains. The United States is Japan's primary trading partner. Commercial exchanges also occur between Japan and China, Indonesia, Taiwan, Australia, Germany, and many other nations.

Workers harvest tea leaves near Kyoto, Japan. By planting on terraced land, farmers make use of hillsides that would not ordinarily be suitable for crops.

Agriculture

Until World War II, many Japanese farmers rented their land, turning over as much as half of their harvests to their landlords. A land-reform program after the war enabled tenant farmers to buy the land they worked. Since then, farms have decreased in size and average only about 4 acres (1.6 hectares). Agriculture accounts for about 2 percent of the gross domestic product and employs 5 percent of the workforce.

Despite the small size of their acreages, Japanese farmers produce high crop yields. Irrigation, improved seeds, chemical fertilizers, and modern machinery have increased harvests. Terracing—cutting level strips of land out of hillsides—adds to the area of land that can be cultivated. Throughout much of the country, the weather permits two or more plantings a year, and farmers are able to meet about three-quarters of the nation's food requirements.

More than one-third of the land cultivated in Japan is devoted to rice, the country's most important crop. Other crops include wheat, barley, soybeans, potatoes, sweet potatoes, sugar beets, cabbages, tea, and tobacco. Fruits include mandarin oranges, apples, pears, and grapes. Since Japanese diets have expanded to include more American and European foods, farmers have also begun to raise chickens, hogs, and beef and dairy cattle, but grazing land is limited.

With only about 15 percent of Japan's land suitable for cultivation, government policy aids farmers so that they can produce as much food as possible. In the past, Japan did not import rice unless bad weather severely reduced the nation's rice harvest, as happened in 1993. Even after restrictions on imports were loosened, high tariffs were often placed on imported rice to support domestic rice production. These and other well-intentioned policies for farmers are sometimes implemented at the expense of the rest of the Japanese, who often end up paying high prices for food.

> Visit vgsbooks.com for links to websites with additional information about Japan's economy. You'll find a link to a converter where you can get the most up-to-date exchange rate and see how many yen are in a U.S. dollar. Other links give detailed information on Japanese agriculture, including rice farming, history, and research.

Fishing

Fish—the primary source of protein in the Japanese diet—is second only to rice as a food staple. As a result, fishing is an important industry in Japan, although industrial pollution has reduced the catch.

Japan's fishing industry is the largest in the world. Thousands of vessels take in more than 6 million tons (5.4 million metric tons) of seafood yearly. The catch is so large because the cold Oyashio and warm Kuroshio Currents converge near Cape Inubo off the coast of eastern Honshu. Thus, both cold-water and warm-water species thrive in the coastal waters of Japan.

Japan's catches of tuna and salmon are among the largest in the world. Other fish include mackerel, pollack, sardines, eels, and flatfish. Fishing crews also haul in octopuses, squid, clams, carp, scallops, and shrimp. Oysters and seaweed are cultivated in sea farms along the coast.

Japanese crews also catch whales, despite a ban instituted by the International Whaling Commission. Japan claims to be killing the whales for scientific research rather than for commercial reasons, but whale meat continues to be sold on the Japanese market.

Transportation

Japan's transportation system includes railroads, highways, coastal shipping, and airlines. Although the system is modern and efficient overall, dense urban populations have caused acute traffic congestion, and public transportation within cities is severely overcrowded.

Most of the nation's 17,000 miles (27,353 km) of railways were owned and operated by the government until it sold them to private companies in 1987. The electric Tokaido line's Shinkansen, or bullet-trains, began operation in the 1960s and are capable of speeds of up to 150 miles per hour (241 km/hr). A well-distributed and well-maintained system, Japan's railways handle both passenger and freight traffic. Despite overcrowding, Japanese trains are famous for being on time. More than 700,000 miles (1,126,300 km) of roads serve Japan, and the nation ranks second in the world (behind the United States) in the number of registered passenger cars.

With over 18,000 miles (28,962 km) of coastline, Japan has one of the largest merchant fleets in the world and handles millions of tons of cargo yearly. Coastal shipping is especially important between ports on the Pacific Ocean and the Inland Sea. In addition to the main ports at Chiba, Kobe, and Nagoya, smaller ports service towns and cities all over Japan. Ships carry almost half of the nation's freight, while trucks carry most of the remainder.

Japan Airlines offers international flights from Tokyo to Europe, the United States, Canada, Mexico, the Middle East, and Southeast Asia. Domestic flights connect major cities within Japan. Tokyo and Osaka both have large international airports.

The Future

One of the greatest challenges facing Japan is its struggling economy. Its recovery—and its future—depend largely on achieving a stable government and on establishing and maintaining good international relations, especially in matters of trade. In addition, although the Japanese generally enjoy a high standard of living, severe housing shortages, pollution, stress, and congested traffic all affect the quality of Japanese life. Japan's high population density makes these problems harder to solve. The rapidly growing percentage of elderly in the population is yet another major issue that Japan must address.

Despite the difficulties ahead, Japan has demonstrated a great gift for successful adaptation to new circumstances over the centuries. The country's long history and many strengths give the Japanese people a wealth of resources to call upon as they face the future.

Timeline

CA. 10,000 B.C.	The Jomon culture begins.
CA. 300 B.C.	The Yayoi culture begins.
CA. A.D. 300s	The Yamato culture begins.
A.D. 600s	Buddhism becomes widespread in Japan.
645	The Taika Reform begins.
701	The Taiho law code becomes the first legal system in Japan.
710	A capital is established in Nara.
794	The imperial government moves the capital to Heian-kyo (Kyoto).
858	The Fujiwara clan takes power.
CA. 1000	Lady Murasaki writes *The Tale of Genji*.
1160	The Taira take control from the Fujiwara.
1185	The Minamoto clan takes power, and Yoritomo becomes leader.
1300s	The Noh style of drama develops.
1333	Emperor Go-Daigo and General Ashikaga Takauji take power.
1338	Takauji declares himself shogun.
1467–1477	Onin War between members of Ashikaga shogunate destroys much of Kyoto.
1549	Jesuit priest Francis Xavier arrives in Japan.
1600s	Bunraku and Kabuki styles of drama develop.
CA. 1635	Japan begins limiting contact with outside world.
1693	Poet Matsuo Basho begins his final journey to northern Japan, documented in his book *The Narrow Road to the Deep North*.
1707	The last eruption of Mount Fuji takes place.
CA. 1820s–1830s	Hokusai publishes his wood-block print series *Thirty-Six Views of Mount Fuji*.
1853	Commodore Matthew C. Perry arrives in Japan.
1858	The Japanese sign a trade treaty with Townsend Harris.
1868	Emperor Meiji takes power, and the Meiji Restoration begins. The capital is moved to Edo (Tokyo).
1885	Ito Hirobumi becomes Japan's first prime minister.

1889	The first Japanese constitution is enacted.
1894–1895	First Chinese-Japanese War
1904–1905	Russo-Japanese War
1914–1918	World War I
1931	Japan invades Manchuria.
1937	The second Chinese-Japanese War begins.
1939	World War II begins.
1941	Japanese forces bomb Pearl Harbor, Hawaii.
1942	Battle of Midway
1945	U.S. forces drop atomic bombs on Hiroshima and Nagasaki, and Japan is placed under military occupation by Allies. The second Chinese-Japanese War and World War II end.
1947	Japan's new constitution, drawn up by the Allies, goes into effect.
1952	The Allied occupation of Japan officially ends.
1953	First television broadcasts air in Japan.
1955	Liberal Democratic Party (LDP) is formed.
1964	The Summer Olympics are held in Tokyo. The "bullet train" (Shinkansen) begins service between Tokyo and Osaka.
1968	Kawabata Yasunari becomes the first Japanese author to receive the Nobel Prize for literature.
1972	The Winter Olympics are held in Sapporo.
1985	The yen's value rises in world market.
1993	The LDP loses in national elections, and a new government is formed by several small parties.
1995	The Great Hanshin Earthquake hits Kobe. Poisonous gas is released in the Tokyo subway system by a religious cult.
1998	The Winter Olympics are held in Nagano.
2001	Prime Minister Koizumi Junichiro appoints five women to his cabinet, the most ever appointed in Japanese history.
2002	Japan and South Korea co-host the first World Cup soccer tournament held in Asia.

COUNTRY NAME Nihon (or Nippon) Koku (Land of the Rising Sun)

AREA 145,869 square miles (377,801 square kilometers)

MAIN LANDFORMS Main islands of Honshu, Hokkaido, Kyushu, Shikoku; Ryukyu Islands; Japanese Alps; Mount Fuji

HIGHEST POINT Mount Fuji (12,388 feet, or 3,776 meters above sea level)

LOWEST POINT Sea level

MAJOR RIVERS Ishikari River, Shinano River

ANIMALS Japanese macaques (snow monkeys), brown bears, red foxes, rabbits, cranes, herons

CAPITAL CITY Tokyo

OTHER MAJOR CITIES Yokohama, Osaka, Nagoya, Sapporo, Kyoto, Kobe, Fukuoka, Kawasaki

OFFICIAL LANGUAGE Japanese

MONETARY UNIT Yen

JAPANESE CURRENCY

The basic unit of Japanese currency is the yen. The yen was officially adopted in 1871, when the Meiji administration reformed the national banking system. The Mint Bureau was established for the production of coins in 1871, and paper bills were printed abroad by foreign companies. The Bank of Japan, founded in 1882, issued its first bills in 1885.

Since the adoption of the yen, special coins have been minted to commemorate national events such as the Tokyo Olympic Games in 1964 and the enthronement of Emperor Akihito in 1990. The Japanese also have a special affection for the 5-yen coin because the pronunciation of its name also means "good luck."

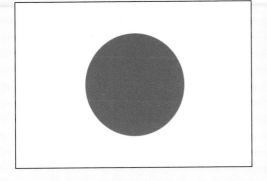

Hinomaru, the Japanese flag features a red circle, representing the rising sun, centered on a white background. The symbol of the red disk is centuries old, and Hinomaru was adopted as the nation's flag in 1870. Since World War II, some controversy has arisen in Japan regarding the negative associations between the flag and Japan's wartime aggression. However, Hinomaru remains a recognized symbol of Japan and its people.

Japan's national anthem is "Kimigayo," translated as "The Emperor's Reign" or "His Majesty's Reign." The author's identity is not known for certain, but the lyrics are from a tanka verse in a tenth-century compilation titled *Kokinshu*. The melody was composed by Hiromori Hayashi in 1880, and by the end of the nineteenth century "Kimigayo" was in regular use at national events and celebrations.

Not all English translations of "Kimigayo" are alike. Two versions are:

> Thousands of years of happy reign be thine;
> Rule on, my lord, till what are pebbles now
> By age united to mighty rocks shall grow
> Whose venerable sides the moss doth line.

> May the reign of the Emperor
> continue for a thousand, nay, eight thousand generations
> and for the eternity that it takes
> for small pebbles to grow into a great rock
> and become covered with moss.

 For a link where you can listen to an instrumental version of Japan's national anthem, "Kimigayo," go to vgsbooks.com.

Japanese names consist of a family name and a personal name. When written in the traditional style, the family name appears first. For example, Minamoto Yoritomo is from the Minamoto family, and his personal name is Yoritomo. Some famous personalities, such as Matsuo Basho, are best known by their personal names, while others are referred to by family name only. The following Japanese names are written in the traditional order, with family name first.

CHIKAMATSU MONZAEMON (1653–1724) Born in what became Fukui prefecture on Honshu Island, Chikamatsu came from a samurai family but entered an artistic rather than a military field. Although this was considered a reduction in social status, Chikamatsu became Japan's greatest playwright. He wrote dozens of Bunraku and Kabuki plays.

FUTABAYAMA SADAJI (1912–1968) Futabayama was born in Oita prefecture on Kyushu Island. He began his sumo career when he was fifteen and became a legend of the sport. In 1937 he earned the rank of Yokozuna, or grand champion, a title that only sixty-seven wrestlers have ever held. Between 1936 and 1939, Futabayama won sixty-nine bouts in a row, setting a record that is still unbroken.

HIROHITO, OR EMPEROR SHOWA (1901–1989) Born in Tokyo, Hirohito became emperor after the death of his father, Yoshihito or Emperor Taisho, in 1926. In a system with a constitution and a parliament, Hirohito had limited power but great symbolic importance. He was the first Japanese emperor to give public speeches and to travel abroad.

ITO HIROBUMI (1841–1909) Born in Yamaguchi prefecture on southern Honshu Island, Ito was a major figure in the Meiji Restoration and the formation of the new Japanese government. He was one of the authors of the Meiji Constitution and served several terms as Japan's prime minister. Ito also served as a resident general in Korea as Japan attempted to annex the nation, and in 1909 he was assassinated by a member of a Korean independence group.

KATSUSHIKA HOKUSAI (1760–1849) Hokusai was born near Edo (Tokyo). He began drawing when he was five years old and grew up to become one of Japan's most famous artists. Especially known for his landscapes, Hokusai was an energetic artist and an eccentric one. He moved dozens of times during his life, had many pseudonyms, and called himself "the old man mad with painting."

KUKAI (774–835) Born near modern-day Zentsuji, Kukai was a Buddhist priest. He began studying Confucianism and Buddhism as a young man, and in 804 he traveled to China. Kukai returned to Japan to found the Shingon sect and to open a monastery. Known after his death as Kobo Daishi, or Great Teacher Kobo, Kukai was also an artist, a poet, and a skilled calligrapher.

KUROSAWA AKIRA (1910–1998) Kurosawa was born in Tokyo. After high school, he studied painting before turning to filmmaking. Kurosawa's use of traditional Japanese elements with new styles from other countries made him Japan's most prominent filmmaker, with such internationally well-known films as *Rashomon* and *The Seven Samurai.*

MATSUO BASHO (1644–1694) Born in Ueno, Basho began his career as a samurai. After his master died, he moved to Edo (Tokyo) and became a poet. He eventually specialized in haiku. Basho's unique style, Zen Buddhist ideals, and gift for depicting a moment clearly and evocatively elevated haiku to a new level in Japanese literature. One of his most famous works, *The Narrow Road to the Deep North*, describes his journey to the northern part of Japan.

MINAMOTO YORITOMO (1147–1199) Yoritomo was Japan's first shogun, beginning a system of military government that lasted until the 1800s. The son of a defeated warrior, Yoritomo was born near Kyoto and lived as an exile from the age of thirteen to thirty-three. In 1180 he joined a rebellion against the government. By 1185 he had built up his own armies, and in 1192 he became a shogun. The Minamoto shogunate remained in power until the 1330s.

MISHIMA YUKIO (1925–1970) Mishima was born in Tokyo and began his career studying law, but his true interest was writing. He published his first book, *Confessions of a Mask*, in 1949. Mishima also took an interest in poli-tics, forming a radical private army called the Shield Society. After an unsuccessful attempt to spur the group to overthrow the government, Mishima committed hara-kiri.

MORI HANAE (b. 1926) Born in rural Shimane prefecture on Honshu Island, Mori studied literature in college but became interested in fashion design after she was married. In 1951 she opened a studio in Tokyo, and before long, she was designing costumes for movies and putting on runway shows. Women who have worn Mori's designs include Nancy Reagan, Hillary Clinton, and Japan's Princess Masako.

MURASAKI SHIKIBU, LADY (ca. 978–ca. 1026) Lady Murasaki was born in Kyoto and lived in the court of Empress Akiko. The exact dates of Lady Murasaki's birth and death are not known, but historians estimate that she wrote her great novel, *The Tale of Genji*, sometime around A.D. 1000.

OE KENZABURO (b. 1935) Oe was born in a small village on Shikoku Island. As a child during World War II, Oe saw Japan in the midst of change. He experienced a big change himself when he left home to study literature at Tokyo University. Oe's early fiction combines legends from his village with the big-city life that he observed in Tokyo. Later works deal with his relationship with his son, who is mentally handicapped. Oe won the Nobel Prize for literature in 1994.

BATCHELOR MEMORIAL MUSEUM, SAPPORO This museum, located in the Botanical Gardens of Hokkaido's largest city, displays a very large collection of Ainu artifacts. The museum is named after John Batchelor, an English missionary who lived in Hokkaido in the 1800s and studied the Ainu people.

DAITOKU-JI TEMPLE, KYOTO A complex of Zen Buddhist temples and monasteries, Daitoku-ji's first buildings were erected in the 1300s. In the 1600s, Daitoku-ji became a center for the tea ceremony, and Senno Rikyu, one of the great masters of the ceremony, is buried there. The Zen garden of the Daisen-in subtemple is famous for its simple and beautiful composition of sand, rocks, and greenery.

HIMEJI CASTLE, HIMEJI A medieval structure that was used by daimyo and samurai until the mid-1800s, Himeji Castle has moats, turrets, and a central tower that looks five stories high but conceals two extra floors. Because of its white walls and graceful appearance, the castle has been nicknamed the "white egret castle" and the "white heron castle."

NARA Nara was Japan's first capital, as well as a stop on the Silk Road trade route. Most of the old city is now a park, the site of temples, shrines, and artifacts—some of which date back to the 600s—and home to hundreds of sacred deer. A few of Nara's treasures are the Kasuga Taisha (a Shinto shrine); the Todai-ji (a Buddhist temple) and its Great Buddha statue over fifty feet high; and Kofuku-ji, a group of buildings that includes two pagodas.

OKINAWA Okinawa was not officially part of Japan until the 1800s and was closely tied to China for centuries. In modern times, Okinawan culture is somewhat different from that of Japan's main islands. Naha, Okinawa's primary city, offers a glimpse into traditional Okinawan music, crafts, and cuisine. Okinawa also has many beautiful natural attractions such as sandy beaches, a large system of caves, and steep cliffs.

PEACE MEMORIAL PARK, HIROSHIMA This park contains a museum and a number of monuments in memory of the victims of the atomic bomb in 1945. Sights include sculptures, the Peace Flame, and the preserved remains of one of the only structures left standing after the bombing.

TOKYO Japan's capital city is a dense metropolis of government buildings, skyscrapers, shrines, temples, and shopping arcades. Just a few of the notable sights are the Imperial Palace, the Diet Building, Tokyo National Museum, Ueno Park, and Senso-ji Temple. Visitors and residents also enjoy dining in Tokyo's many restaurants, and theatres, sporting events, karaoke bars, and other diversions offer plenty of options for entertainment.

Buddhism: one of Japan's two major religions, along with Shinto. Founded in India by the monk Siddhartha Gautama, also known as Buddha, Buddhism arrived in Japan around the sixth century A.D. Some of Buddhism's main ideals are the search for enlightenment and the practice of noble actions.

Confucianism: a system of ethics centered around the teachings of the Chinese philosopher Confucius, who emphasized the necessity of morality and proper conduct in all aspects of life. Confucian thought has influenced many areas of Japanese society, including government and economics.

daimyo: an estate owner who controlled large landholdings that were farmed by peasants and protected by warriors (samurai). Daimyo were free to rule their estates as they pleased, but they were required to serve the shogun and his government. The power of the daimyo was passed down within families.

haniwa: clay figures found in the burial mounds of the Kofun or Yamato period. Some haniwa were simply clay cylinders, but many were shaped like people, animals, houses, and other objects.

hara-kiri: also called seppuku, the ritual of suicide by disembowelment. Samurai found guilty of crimes or offenses were often condemned to commit hara-kiri, which was considered a more honorable death than execution.

League of Nations: established in 1920, an international alliance of countries to prevent war. The League of Nations was officially dismantled in 1946, and its duties came under the jurisdiction of the United Nations.

samurai: a Japanese warrior. The samurai began as members of private armies, serving both the daimyo and the shogun. They eventually grew into a powerful class of their own and lived by a code of honor that demanded bravery, duty, and fierce loyalty. In addition to being skilled in battle, samurai were expected to be educated enough to read and write.

Shinto: Japan's native religion, whose ancient origins are unknown. Shinto's central feature is the belief in many spirits or forces (kami) that reside in nature and affect human existence. The entrance to every Shinto shrine is marked by a torii, or gate, constructed of two posts, symbolizing pillars holding up the sky, and two connecting horizontal bars, symbolizing the earth.

shoen: a privately controlled, untaxed estate. Shoen were not subject to the legislation of the government, and the samurai armies of large estates often fought with each other to gain more power and land for estate owners.

shogun: a military leader, whose government was called a shogunate. Although shoguns were officially servants of the emperor, their power usually exceeded that of the imperial government. Leadership of the shogunate was passed down within families or clans.

Soka Gakkai: founded in 1930, an influential religious organization based on the strict Nichiren Shoshu sect of Japanese Buddhism. Soka Gakkai also started the Komeito, a political party that maintains a following of millions.

zaibatsu: large business conglomerates spanning diverse areas of the economy, including agriculture, manufacturing, and banking. In general, single families owned and controlled zaibatsu. After World War II, the zaibatsu broke into independent companies, many of which remained very successful.

Glossary

Selected Bibliography

Benson, John, et. al. *Japan,* **New York: Dorling Kindersley, 2000.**
This illustrated travel guide provides historical and cultural details along with practical information for visitors to Japan.

***CNN.com Asia.* Asia.**
Website: <http://asia.cnn.com> (Feb. 13, 2001).
This site provides current events and breaking news about Japan, as well as a searchable archive of older articles.

Cortazzi, Sir Hugh. *Modern Japan: A Concise Survey.* **New York: St. Martin's Press, 1993.**
This book offers an overview of Japanese history, geography, and culture, followed by a more detailed look at the economy, politics, and government of twentieth-century Japan.

***The Europa World Year Book 2000.* London: Europa Publications Limited, 2000.**
This annual publication covers Japan's recent history, economy, and government, as well as providing a wealth of statistics on population, employment, trade, and more. A short directory of offices and organizations is also included.

Henshall, Kenneth G. *A History of Japan: From Stone Age to Superpower.* **New York: St. Martin's Press, 1999.**
This book offers a detailed, chronological history of Japan, from prehistoric times to the end of the twentieth century.

Japan Travel Bureau. *A Look Into Japan: Illustrated.* **Tokyo: Japan Travel Bureau, 1993.**
Part of the Japan in Your Pocket series published by the Japan Travel Bureau, this introduction to Japanese culture includes tidbits on religion, traditional arts and crafts, hobbies, food, clothing, and more.

Japan Travel Bureau. *Who's Who of Japan: 100 Historical Personages.* **Tokyo: Japan Travel Bureau, 1990.**
This volume in the Japan in Your Pocket series provides brief biographies of notable figures in Japanese history, from monks and haiku poets to shoguns and samurai.

Kinoshita, June and Nicholas Palevsky. *Gateway to Japan.* **New York: Kodansha International, 1998.**
This in-depth travel guide includes informative sections on Japanese history, religion, art, food, festivals, and people.

Library of Congress, Federal Research Division
Japan: A Country Study.
Website: <http://lcweb2.loc.gov/frd/cs/jptoc.html>
This title gives a moderately detailed overview of Japan's government, economy, history, society, and arts.

New York Times. *The New York Times on the Web.*
website: <http://www.nytimes.com> (Feb. 13, 2001).
This searchable site provides online access to articles from the *New York Times.*

Population Reference Bureau
Website: <http://www.prb.org> (Feb. 13, 2001).
This annual statistics sheet provides a wealth of data on Japan's population, birth and death rates, fertility rate, infant mortality rate, and other useful demographic information.

Sugimoto Yoshio. *An Introduction to Japanese Society.* New York: Cambridge University Press, 1997.
This title provides an analysis of Japanese society, from employment and education to family and social life.

Tames, Richard. *A Traveller's History of Japan.* New York: Interlink Books, 1993.
This book surveys Japanese history, with an emphasis on society and culture.

Tanaka Yoshio, ed. *Japan As It Is: A Bilingual Guide.* Tokyo: Gakken, 1990.
This book offers brief descriptions of many aspects of Japanese life and society, with a focus on cultural information.

Turner, Barry, ed. *The Statesman's Yearbook: The Politics, Cultures, and Economics of the World, 2001.* New York: Macmillan Press, 2000.
This resource provides concise information on Japanese history, climate, government, economy, and culture, including relevant statistics.

Varley, Paul. *Japanese Culture.* Honolulu: University of Hawaii Press, 2000.
This title surveys Japanese arts and other cultural expressions and analyzes their roles in the nation's society and history.

Addiss, Stephen. *The Art of Zen: Paintings and Calligraphy by Japanese Monks, 1600–1925.* **New York: H. N. Abrams, 1989.**
This book presents the work of Japanese Zen Buddhist monks spanning over three hundred years, combined with historical information and biographies of some of the artists.

Cook, Harry. *Samurai: The Story of a Warrior Tradition.* **New York: Sterling Publishing, 1993.**
This book presents a wealth of details about samurai life and history, including weapons, battles, beliefs, and the effect of the samurai culture on modern Japan.

Cook, Haruko Taya, and Theodore F. Cook, eds. *Japan at War: An Oral History.* **New York: New Press, 1992.**
This collection of essays recounts the World War II memories and experiences of soldiers and civilians from all over Japan, covering topics from Hiroshima to daily life during wartime.

Finley, Carol. *Art of Japan: Wood-Block Color Prints.* **Minneapolis: Lerner Publications Company, 1998.**
This illustrated introduction to the art of ukiyo-e discusses the form's history and technique and offers descriptions of major artists and subjects.

Heinrichs, Ann. *Japan.* **Danbury, CT: Children's Press, 1998.**
This book presents a summary of Japanese geography, people, society, and culture.

Hoobler, Dorothy, and Thomas Hoobler. *Showa: The Age of Hirohito.* **New York: Walker and Company, 1990.**
This biography covers the life of Emperor Hirohito and the great changes in Japan during his long reign.

Katsuichi Honda. *Harukor: An Ainu Woman's Tale.* **Translated by Kyoko Selden. Los Angeles: University of California Press, 2000.**
Although the Harukor of the title is a fictional character, her story is based on extensive research on Ainu society and daily life. The first part of the book offers an explanation of Ainu history and culture.

Kawabata Yasunari. *First Snow on Fuji.* **Translated by Michael Emmerich. Washington, D.C.: Counterpoint, 1999.**
This collection of short stories by Japan's first winner of the Nobel Prize for literature is a series of glimpses into the lives of Japanese men and women, from love and romance to careers.

Matsuo Basho. *The Narrow Road to Oku.* **Translated by Donald Keene. New York: Kodansha International, 1997.**
This translation (also called *Narrow Road to the North*) of Basho's journal and haiku collection documenting his journey to northern Japan presents the text in English and Japanese with illustrations by Masayuki Miyata.

Natsume Soseki. *I Am a Cat.* **Translated by Aiki Ito and Graeme Wilson. Rutland, VT: Charles E. Tuttle, 1972.**
Originally published in Japan in 1911, this novel is told from the point of view of a housecat, observing life and society around him in Meiji-era Japan.

Further Reading and Websites

Netzley, Patricia D. *Japan.* **San Diego, CA: Lucent Books, 2000.**
This book provides an overview of Japan's geography, economy, government, culture, and history.

Poisson, Barbara Aoki. *The Ainu of Japan.* **Minneapolis: Lerner Publications Company, 2002.**
This book describes the modern and traditional cultural practices and economies of the Ainu. It also discusses the history of the Ainu in Japan.

Ross, Floys Hiatt. *Shinto: The Way of Japan.* **Boston: Beacon Press, 1965. Reprint, Westport, CT: Greenwood Press, 1983.**
This book discusses the history, beliefs, practices, and shrines of the Shinto religion in Japan. A brief section also addresses the place of Shinto in modern Japanese society.

Streissguth, Tom. *Japan.* **Minneapolis: Carolrhoda Books, 1997.**
This book takes readers on an entertaining tour of Japan's land, society, and culture.

Tanaka Sen'o, and Tanaka Sendo. *The Tea Ceremony.* **New York: Kodansha International, 1998.**
This book introduces the Japanese tea ceremony, including its history, meaning, and practice.

vgsbooks.com
Website: <http://www.vgsbooks.com>
Visit vgsbooks.com, the homepage of the Visual Geography Series®. You can get linked to all sorts of useful on-line information, including geographical, historical, demographic, cultural, and economic websites. The vgsbooks.com site is a great resource for late-breaking news and statistics.

Weston, Mark. *Giants of Japan: The Lives of Japan's Most Influential Men and Women.* **New York: Kodansha International, 1999.**
This book provides brief biographies of over thirty major figures in Japanese history, politics, arts, and entertainment.

Weston, Reiko. *Cooking the Japanese Way.* **Minneapolis: Lerner Publications, 2002.**
This cultural cookbook presents recipes for a variety of authentic and traditional Japanese dishes, including special foods for holidays and festivals.

Yoshimoto Banana. *Kitchen.* **Translated by Megan Backus. New York: Grove Press, 1993.**
This award-winning novel, by one of Japan's most popular current authors, is a look at the life of a young woman in modern Tokyo.

Yumoto Kazumi. *The Friends.* **Translated by Cathy Hirano. New York: Farrar Straus Giroux, 1996.**
This novel follows the lives of best friends, Kiyama, Kawabe, and Yamashita during the summer before they take their school entrance exams. When Yamashita's grandmother dies, it sparks the boys' curiosity about death. As they try to understand death, they learn a valuable lesson about living.

Index

agriculture, 5, 9, 12, 13, 14, 21, 26, 63–64
Ainu, 40–41
artists, 5, 7, 52, 54, 70
Ashikaga shogunate, 25–27, 66
Ashikaga Takauji, General, 25, 66
authors, 5, 24, 51–52, 66, 67, 70–71

Bonin Islands, 8, 14, 27, 35
Buddhism, 22, 49, 50, 54, 66
Bunraku, 52, 70
burakumin, 39–40

China, 8, 9, 20, 22, 29, 30–31, 38, 49, 62
Chinese-Japanese War, 29, 67
cities, 8, 12, 14, 17–19, 26, 37, 38, 66, 67, 72
climate, 15–16
Confucianism, 22, 48
currency, 68

daimyo, 24, 25, 26, 28
domestic challenges, 35–37, 47, 65
drama, 52–53, 66
dress, 57

earthquakes, 9, 13; Great Hanshin Earthquake, 36, 67; Great Kanto Earthquake, 30
East China Sea, 8, 14
economy, 5, 35–37, 58–65
education, 45–46
emperors, 5, 20, 23, 25, 33, 37, 66
environment, 18, 37, 46, 65
Era of Warring States, 25

famous people, 70–71
fauna, 17
festivals. *See* holidays
fishing, 17, 64
flag, 69
flora, 16–17
food, 9, 10, 56–57, 58
forests, 9, 17
Fujiwara leadership, 23–25, 66
Fujiyama (Mount Fuji), 10, 66
Fukuoka, 19

Go-Daigo, 25, 66

government, 37, 66, 67

health, 18, 46–47
Heian period, 23, 25
Hidaka Mountains, 12
Hirohito (emperor), 32, 70
Hiroshima, 19, 32, 67, 72
history: archaeological finds, 20; Ashikaga shogunate, 25–27, 66; Chinese influence, 22–23, 26; World Wars I and II, 29–32; Fujiwara leadership, 23–25, 66; Japanese imperialism, 29; Jomon civilization, 20, 66; Kamakura period, 25; Meiji Restoration, 5, 28–29, 66; military occupation, 32–33, 67; Minamoto family, 25, 66, 71; modern, 35–37; postwar boom, 34–35; prehistory, 20–21; Taika Reform, 22, 23, 24, 66; Taira family, 25, 66; Tokugawa shogunate, 27–28, 51, 54; Yamato culture, 21, 66; Yayoi culture, 21, 39, 66
Hokkaido, 8, 12, 15, 16, 17, 27, 41
holidays and festivals, 15, 17, 42, 50–51, 57
Honshu, 8, 10, 12, 14, 15, 16, 17, 19, 32, 64

Inland Sea, 13, 19, 65
Ishikari Mountains, 12
Ishikari River, 12, 15
Ito Hirobumi, 29, 70

Japan: boundaries, location, and size, 8–9; cities, 8, 12, 14, 17–19, 26, 37, 38, 66, 67; climate, 15–16; domestic challenges, 35–37, 47, 65; economy, 5, 35–37, 58–65; environment, 18, 37, 46, 65; flora and fauna, 16–17; future, 65; government, 37, 66, 67; history, 20–37; holidays and festivals, 15, 17, 42, 50–51, 57; industrialization, 58–62; isolation, 4–5, 27, 41, 66; maps, 6, 11; outside influences, 4, 7, 27, 29, 53; population, 10, 12, 13, 14, 38, 41; religion, 20, 22, 49, 50, 54, 66; rivers and lakes, 14–15
Japanese Alps, 10

juku, 45

Kabuki, 52, 53, 70
Kamakura period, 25
kamikaze, 25
Kanto Plain, 10
Kobe, 8, 18, 36, 65, 67
Koizumi Junichiro, 37
Korea, 8, 9, 20, 22, 29, 49
Korea Strait, 8
Kushiro Plain, 12
Kyoto, 8, 18, 23, 25, 28, 32, 50, 66, 72
Kyushu, 8, 12, 14, 15, 17, 19, 25, 26, 32

language, 41–42
literature, 24, 51–52

maps, 6, 11
marriage and family, 44
Matsuyama, 19
Meiji Restoration, 5, 28–29, 51, 66
Michinaga, 24
Minamoto family, 25, 66, 71
mineral resources, 9, 59
modernization, 29
monsoons, 15, 16
Mount Fuji. *See* Fujiyama
music, 53

Nagasaki, 32, 67
Nagoya, 19, 65
nakodo, 42, 44
Nara, 23, 66, 72
national anthem, 69
Nihon (Land of the Rising Sun), 4, 22
Niigata Plain, 10, 15
Nippon. *See* Nihon
Noh, 52

Okayama, 19
Okinawa, 14, 36–37, 72
onsen (mineral springs), 13
Osaka, 8, 18–19, 21, 60, 65, 67
Osaka Bay, 19
Osaka Plain, 10

Pacific Ocean, 4, 8, 10, 14, 16, 65
people, 38–41
Perry, Commodore Matthew C., 26, 66
pollution. *See* environment

population, 10, 12, 13, 14, 38, 41

religion, 19, 20, 22, 26, 48–50, 54, 66
Russia, 9, 27, 28, 29
Russo-Japanese War, 29, 67
Ryukyu Islands, 8, 14, 27, 29, 35

samurai, 24–25, 27, 29, 52
Sapporo, 15, 19, 67, 72
Sea of Japan, 8, 10, 16
Shikoku, 8, 13, 15, 16, 17
Shinto, 20, 22, 49, 50
shogun, 25, 66
Shotoku, Prince, 22, 23
social structure, 42–43
sports and recreation, 55–56

Taika Reform, 22, 23, 24, 66
Taira family, 25, 66
Taiwan, 14, 29, 62
tea ceremony, 57
Tojo Hideki, 31, 32
Tokugawa Ieyashu, 27
Tokugawa shogunate, 27–28, 51, 54
Tokyo, 8, 10, 16, 17–18, 27, 28, 30,
    36, 38, 46, 60, 65, 66, 67, 72
Tokyo Bay, 18, 32
Toyotomi Hideyoshi, 26–27
trade, 5, 26, 27, 30, 59, 62–63
transportation, 64–65
Treaty of Mutual Cooperation and
    Security, 34
tsunami, 9

United States, 27, 28, 31–35, 37–38,
    58, 62, 65; Pearl Harbor, Hawaii,
    31, 67

volcanoes, 9–10, 13–14

World War I, 29–30, 67
World War II, 7, 25, 31–32, 33,
    34–35, 42, 52, 58, 60, 63, 67

Yamato culture, 21, 66
Yayoi culture, 21, 39, 66
Yokohama, 8, 18, 30
Yoritomo, 25, 71

zaibatsu, 29, 30, 33

Captions for photos appearing on cover and chapter openers:

Cover: The Japanese Alps provide the perfect backdrop for the Matsumoto Castle in central Honshu.

pp. 4–5 A torii gate stands in the Inland Sea off the coast of Honshu. A torii is a gateway, commonly used at the entrance to a Shinto shrine.

pp. 8–9 The Japanese Alps ring a lake on the island of Honshu.

pp. 38–39 Schoolchildren mug for a photographer.

pp. 48–49 Wearing traditional dress and makeup, geisha (traditional Japanese female entertainers) perform a dance at the annual Spring Festival in Kyoto.

pp. 58–59 Japanese autoworkers assemble automobiles at the Nissan Motor Company, headquartered in Tokyo.

Photo Acknowledgments
The images in this book are used with the permission of: Paul J. Buklarewicz, pp. 4–5, 13, 14, 15, 22, 52–53, 53 (top), 54; PresentationMaps.com, pp. 6, 11; © Cameramann International, Ltd., pp. 8–9, 18–19, 26, 27, 28, 30, 40, 41, 43, 44, 45, 46, 47 (top), 50, 57, 58–59, 61; Minneapolis Public Library & Information Center, p. 10; © Michael S. Yamashita/CORBIS, pp. 12, 55; © Lloyd Cluff/CORBIS, p. 16; © Superstock, pp. 17, 36, 47 (bottom), 48–49, 63; © Bettmann/CORBIS, pp. 23, 29, 35; © Asian Art & Archaeology, Inc./ CORBIS, p. 24 (top); © Sakamoto Photo Research Laboratory/CORBIS, p. 24 (bottom); National Archives, pp. 31, 32, 33; Independent Picture Service, p. 34; © Elaine Little/World Photo Images, pp. 38–39; Japan National Tourist Organization, p. 51; © American Lutheran Church; used by permission of Augsburg Fortress, p. 60; Todd Strand/Independent Picture Service, p. 68; Laura Westlund, p. 69.

Cover photo: © Cameramann International, Ltd. Back cover photo: NASA.